AXIS OF HOPE

AXIS
of
HOPE

A PROSPECTIVE FOR COMMUNITY

CENTRIC GOVERNMENT FOR

IRAN AND OTHER MENA COUNTRIES

Kamal Y. Azari

February 2014

The library congress has cataloged this edition as follow:
Kamal Y. Azari

Library of Congress Control Number: 2014902639

Cover Design by Glen Edelstein

Book design by Glen Edelstein

ISBN: 061596494X
ISBN 13: 9780615964942

Lumma Press, Petaluma, CA

P O Box 1089
Petaluma CA, 94952
lummapress@gmail.com

Printed in the United States of America

ACKNOWLEDGMENTS

The ideas that shaped this book came to mind while the fever of political change was sweeping the Islamic world and the Iran 21 conference of young professionals was gathering at the Stevens Institute of Technology to explore desirable forms of government and the role of government in modern society. The diversity of opinions and the range of conflicting ideas among the highly educated and professional young Iranians at Iran 21 became the impetus for writing this book. I cannot find words to show my appreciation for each participant and their individual contributions to this project.

Although I had been out of academia for many decades, my training as an engineer and political scientist, and later in life my many entrepreneurial adventures, allowed me a unique perspective on this subject. However, I am indebted for the help and support of so many people, especially my friend Dr. Ali Mostashari, director of the Center for Complex Adaptive Sociotechnological Systems at Stevens, who graciously invited me to Iran 21 and later collaborated closely with me in refining my ideas. In fact, Dr. Mostashari wrote several pages of the first draft of chapter four as coauthor, and I am sure this book would have been much more if his busy life had allowed him to be a coauthor as it was originally planned. In any case, I am grateful for all his help and support.

The Saturday night forums at the home of Nahid Ziaee and my friend Ahmad Mirfakhari were very helpful in refining my ideas. I am truly grateful for the intelligent critiques of all participants, which have enriched me beyond words. Special thanks go to Morteza Negahi, who has always helped me by being the contrarian and sharpening my arguments. I never had the opportunity to express my deepest gratitude for the wealth of knowledge that I received from the late Dr. Mohamad Jafer Mahjoub. He gave me a unique sense for appreciating history with intellectual curiosity, which helped me in a way that words alone cannot express.

I cannot begin to fully appreciate the support of my family, especially my wife, Parichehr who has tolerated me during this period. Special thanks to my brother, Shojs Azari who read and commented on the first daft of this book. The help and support of Lee Ann Osbun provided essential research for some of this work. Gary Miller's sharp and precise editing skills made this work more readable and easier to follow, as did Bob Anderson's editorial comments.

I have never had the opportunity to publicly express my enormous gratitude to my mentor John Enletis, chair of the Political Science Department and director of Middle East Studies at Fordham University. I will do so now. Without his help and support, I would have never graduated or even dared to write these pages. Finally, Fordham University's invitation to be the speaker for the spring Gannon Lecture on March 30, 2012, allowed me for the first time to talk about this model at such a prestigious gathering. I truly appreciate this amazing boost to my stamina, which helped me to complete this project.

I am truly indebted to Fordham for many other reasons as well.

This institution not only trained me, but their continued support has helped me in this project and many others. I wish someday to show my deepest gratitude. I am especially grateful to Nancy A. Busch, the dean of the Graduate School of Arts and Sciences, and especially Father McShane, the president of Fordham, for all their kind support and encouragements. I truly feel privileged to have such family. Thank you.

Kamal Y. Azari
Petaluma, 2013

"It was the best of times, it was the worst of times, it was the age of wisdom, it was the age of foolishness, it was the epoch of belief, it was the epoch of incredulity, it was the season of Light, it was the season of Darkness, it was the spring of hope, it was the winter of despair, we had everything before us, we had nothing before us, we were all going direct to Heaven, we were all going direct the other way. . . ."

— Charles Dickens, *A Tale of Two Cities*

CONTENTS

ACKNOWLEDGMENTS   v

PREFACE   1

INTRODUCTION   7

Chapter One:
INTRODUCTION TO IRANIAN HISTORY
A New Interpretation   13

    The Development of the Aryan Narrative   15

    The Emergence of Iran — Cyrus the Great and Darius
    the Great, the Founding Fathers   18

    The Sasanian Dynasty   23

    The Evolution of Islam   25

    The Islamification of Iran   29

    Plato's Academy in Exile   30

    Hasan of Basra   35

    Characteristics of Islamic Culture   44

    A Serious Challenge to Rational Thinking   48

Internal Change   56

The European Impact   57

The New Iran   61

Chapter Two:

A BRIEF HISTORY OF THE MODERN STATE   63

The Rise of Europe and the End of the Islamic

Golden Age   63

Emergence of the Modern State   65

Eighteenth Century France   66

The Spirit of the Laws and the Separation of Powers   68

The Founding of the United States   71

Basic Principles of the United States Constitution   76

Chapter Three:

THE MODERN STATE AT A CROSSROAD   83

The Modern State and Corporate Rights   85

Sovereignty, Human Rights, and Regionalization   88

The Changing Nature of War and Conflict   91

Manifestations of Inequality   92

Declining Public Confidence   96

The Brink of Crisis?   98

Creativity, Innovation, and Community   100

A Vision for Change   104

Chapter Four:

**COMMUNITY, HUMAN CREATIVITY, AND
DEMOCRACY: MANIFESTO FOR A
COMMUNITY-CENTRIC GOVERNMENT**   107

Introduction   107

Participatory Democracy Versus Liberal Democracy   111

Iran and MENA: An Ideal Opportunity 113

Principles of the Community-Centric Governance
Structure 114

Government Structure and Responsibilities 115

National Government 116

Executive Branch 117

Legislative Branch 117

Federal Judicial Branch 118

The National Wealth Trust Branch 118

Local Community Government (see Figure 1 at
end of chapter) 122

Trust Networks and the Success of Community-Centric
Governance 124

Trust Networks, Bargaining, and the Creation
of Democracy 127

An Unprecedented Opportunity 131

Figure 1:
STRUCTURE OF COMMUNITY-CENTRIC
GOVERNMENT 132

CONCLUSION 135

NOTES 141

BIBLIOGRAPHY 151

APPENDIX 158

INDEX 165

PREFACE

The first modern states arose in the beginning of nineteenth century. At the time, the world's population was about one billion, and most of the Earth's natural resources remained untapped. Since then, the modern state has employed people to use their creativity and ingenuity to exploit those resources. The political system, and the modern sociopolitical model, functions through the allocation of economic scarcities: modern systems allocate economic scarcity based on the capabilities of the individual participants. Scarcity forces people to make choices, which drives the economy. Yet the model only works if the economy continuously expands to allocate more scarcities. Otherwise, economic activity will stop.

In the past two hundred years we have witnessed profound changes in the socioeconomic conditioning of human life. Among many other changes, new terminology has entered the human lexicon: *recession* and *depression.* These words bring terror to the people of today, just as *famine* and *war* have and still do. To avoid recession and depression, the system mobilizes the population for a continuous orgy of consumption: people buy the things they don't need with the money they don't have to keep an economic downturn at bay. Once every few years the bubble bursts. Recession — or worse, depression — occurs, and the system demands human sacrifices. Depending upon the situation, 10, 15, or sometimes 30 percent of the people will lose everything they own, with consequent human suffering on an incredible scale. Then after a few years, the cycle begins again.

The economic system requires constant expansion and the exploitation of natural resources to create more scarce goods. Yet if more goods are created, there must be more demand to consume them. If demand decreases, there is a decrease in economic activity, and the system cannot be sustained.

According to some models, Earth's population will start declining by the year 2060. Today, in many regions, demand has already begun to shrink due to population decline. The population of most European countries is declining rapidly, and Japan will lose half its population in the next eighty years. Some of the nations that have managed to avoid economic harm have done so by exporting capabilities to less developed nations whose population is increasing. But in general, lower population means decreased demand, decreased economic activity, and constant recession, which is what we have witnessed in Japan for the past twenty years and in Europe for the past five.

In the twenty-first century, a number of other factors will impact the world economy. Businesses will increase the use of robotics in economic production, meaning less demand for human workers. Earth's natural abundance will continue to decline, making raw materials more costly. And environmental sustainability issues will constrain economic growth. While a few billionaires such as Bill Gates have begun to return their earned money to the public in the form of charitable investments, many of the world's most wealthy and powerful have used their economic power to buy more of the political process and change the rules even more in their favor. Amid all this change, the future is impossible to predict. However, one thing is clear: the era of rapid economic expansion is ending.

The situation is even more difficult for countries with developing economies. The sociopolitical institutions in developed countries have had the opportunity to evolve for the past two hundred years. Many social experiments, both positive and painful, have refined their cultures, and these nations have functional civil societies, with numerous nongovernmental organizations (NGOs) and strong judicial systems. However, in the newly emerging countries, creating civil societies and establishing the rule of law is a very difficult process and may be an impossible task for nations struggling against a global economic downturn. This raises a critical question: During a constant economic recession or depression, will it be possible for undeveloped countries to advance using the current model of modern government? If not, a new model is needed.

If we are given the opportunity to design a new political model for a nation, how might we improve on the current model? One cannot deny the amazing achievements that modern political systems have granted humanity. They have given reign to individual creativity and ingenuity as the main drivers of human growth. More important, the modern model has shaped individual consciousness and bestowed the capacity to live free as a powerful person based on one's desires.

Any future political model that undermines in any form the power of the individual to live in freedom will not function as an alternative and is doomed to fail. Individual achievement and the desire to be free is now a universal demand. One reason is technology. Today, technology enables human consciousness to travel across cultural and political boundaries at amazing speed, and its power is reflected in the drive for freedom worldwide, from the barrios of Brazil to the Arab Spring.

The modern state has also brought meaning to social organizations and has helped us to develop and understand human consciousness. The ideal philosophical discourses of a few centuries ago have become public common sense. Crucial political information, once the province of a small coterie of society, has become broadly available. The contributions of modern politics are so enormous that we cannot begin to comprehend their impact on human life, and the basis of any political system must be firmly based on that which has come before.

In the pages of this book, we will present a new model for government that maximizes the potential for human growth while freeing people from the threat of constant economic havoc. To construct this model, we will analyze the historical structure and function of the modern government and build a new structure and function based on the following principles:

1. Individual creativity, ingenuity, endurance, and entrepreneurship are the engines of economic growth and prosperity.
2. Individual growth requires the personal freedom to express oneself and to live in a community that supports growth in its own unique way.
3. Combining executive political power and wealth will cause corruption in the political power structure.
4. Absolute power brings absolute corruption.

Although its civic society is not fully developed yet and its judicial branch is not independent and strong, Iran is a natural candidate for such a new political system. The historical and cultural position of Iran in the Middle East and North Africa (MENA) gives Iran a unique opportunity to foster social change and lead the way to a new form of government. At the core of Iran's strength is a characteristic it shares with other MENA nations: strong social trust networks. These networks will form the foundation upon which a responsive, locally based government can be built.

According to Ian Morris[1], new forms of social order start from the most disadvantaged communities; what he calls the advantage of the disadvantaged. Along with North Korea, Iran is one of the most politically and socially disadvantaged countries of the world. Yet its human resources, natural wealth, and strategic geopolitical location combined with the power of technology to connect to the rest of the world make Iran uniquely positioned as a laboratory of democracy.

Iran is composed of about 300 congressional districts, each with a population of 250,000 to 300,000 people. For the past thirty years, there has been a strong tradition of voting participation. The level of corruption is relatively low and voter participation is high. There is a strong political cohesiveness and cooperation among trust networks. Election participants usually cooperate, and the community usually accepts election results without resorting to violence.

Further, Iran has accumulated an amazing amount of national wealth in the office of its leader, much of it from the sale of public resources and the confiscation of wealth from members of the former regime. This national wealth, when properly managed in a public trust fund, would provide critical support for a broadly accessible economy, something that is largely lacking in Iran and in most developing countries today.

For this reason, it is the position of this writer that a new model of government must include a fourth branch at the federal level, the National Trust Fund Branch. The inclusion of this fourth branch of government is the key that will enable the MENA nations to fully develop even during a time of economic decline.

It is important to remember that large-scale political change is never easy. In Iran, obstacles to change include deep schisms within Iranian communities. In addition, Iran's urbanization occurred in a relatively short period of time. As a result, earlier urbanized groups consider those more recently urbanized to be uncivilized, and have contempt for them.

The major gap however, is in the inaccurate and self-serving historical interpretations of Iran's long and complicated history. For centuries, Iranians have adopted the Eurocentric view that their nation has made scant contribution to world culture, when nothing could be further from the truth. Understanding Iran's actual history on a personal level proves very empowering for individuals and is critical in order for large-scale political awareness and for the development of a new consciousness, one in which Iran and its people can once again become a leader in political, economic, and cultural innovation. The first step to creating a new political model is to part the shroud of myth and to reveal the truth about Iran's history.

INTRODUCTION

In the aftermath of the Iranian Green Movement in 2009 and the Arab Spring of 2010, the Middle East and North Africa (MENA) region has embarked on a new chapter in its history. The fall of and challenges to dictatorships in the region have led to serious questions about the development of future democratic governance models that would harmonize with the region's rich history and culture.

Iran and other MENA nations are at a crossroads in regard to shaping their future civilizations. Early indications, particularly in the case of Islamic resurgence in Egypt and the subsequent military coup, show that a direct adoption of Western models of democratic government may prove disastrous in MENA, where many nations lack a vibrant civil society and a strong history of the rule of law.

In this heightened era of uncertainty, the need to explore and understand the region's identity and historical dynamics is a crucial step toward a future that includes an organic and genuine native democracy. Once a cradle of civilization and a center of scientific, cultural, and artistic contributions to humanity, the MENA region has experienced centuries of social and cultural stagnation.

With this new awakening across the region, MENA once again

has the opportunity to change course and revitalize its societies, allowing it to regain its stature as a prime contributor to the growth and creativity of human civilization.

However, mere replication of the Western conception of the modern state will not result in a resurgence of culture in Iran or in MENA, because the modern state itself is in deep crisis. The absence of a robust civil society and the rule of law make such a replication even more unfeasible, dangerous, and dysfunctional. To find a way forward from the current crisis, we need to explore the past and understand what contributed to the stagnation of our societies, which once were vibrant, dynamic, and a source of pride for their citizens. Yet conventional and popularly accepted understandings of MENA's past fail to provide us with a clear understanding of our identity. In fact, ambiguities about MENA's past have resulted in the very cause of its historical demise to be misconstrued as the source of its identity.

In this book, we will limit our analysis to a case study of Iran. Yet the same trends are also evident in many other MENA nations. In fact, for a solution to be sustainable for any country in the region, it must be compatible with the region's history as a whole. For this reason, the governance model proposed in this book is designed to be applicable to other MENA countries. In subsequent works, we will expand the analysis to case studies of other nations in the MENA region.

In Chapter 1, we will analyze Iran's past through the lens of state formation and social transformation. Starting with the Orientalist perspective on Iran's history as conceived in the West during the nineteenth century, the chapter examines Iran from its founding during the reign of Cyrus (fifth century BCE) and the resulting social transformations that over the subsequent twelve centuries culminated in the emergence of an economically powerful, culturally resplendent Islamic state. In this Iranian Golden Age, values such as tolerance of diversity and individual creativity contributed to a social dynamism and prosperity. Yet the introduction of intolerant religious legal interpretations of sharia led to a rapid decline from which Iran has never emerged.

In Chapter 2, we will reexamine the foundations and the development of the modern state in the West. One of the unfortunate consequences of the experience of colonization and imperialism in the MENA region has been the emotional rejection of an objective analysis of the modern state. In the minds of many MENA intellectuals and thought leaders, the modern state has become synonymous with a brutally expansionist, domineering ideology. This one-dimensional viewpoint has inhibited an objective examination of the modern state's strengths and weaknesses, and the genuine learning that can come from such an examination. A clear reevaluation of the experience of the modern state in the West is critical to our fundamental understanding of the political possibilities for democratic governance in MENA.

As exemplified by the United States, the modern political state emerged as a new model of governance based on the European political experience of the post-Enlightenment era. The system was designed with many aspects that for the first time made the individual pursuit of happiness a central tenet of national governance. As such, it created a rich set of mechanisms to ensure individual liberty and allow the individual to determine his or her own destiny.

In Chapter 3, we look at the historical performance of the modern state, and its eventual failure to meet the challenges of a changing economic and technological landscape. Rapid industrialization, coupled with concentration of wealth within the hands of a few, led to the loss of the democratic spirit within the modern state, reducing democracy to the ability to cast ballots every four years rather than the genuine engagement of the citizenry. This chapter analyzes the reasons for these dynamics and maps out the challenges facing the existential modern state in the near future.

Chapter 4 identifies ways to overcome the shortcomings of the modern state, employing a new model for democratic governance that puts people, their creativity, and local communities at the center. We will present a new model for community-centric governance in Iran and analyze its potential based on the insights gained through the analysis of Iranian history.

The model proposes the replacement of the current, highly centralized and repressive state with a system that relies on trust networks and existing community-based structures to create a truly democratic governance structure at the local level. Such a governance structure will enable communities to leverage the creativity of individuals for the greater public good and allow more adaptive and resilient governance mechanisms to take root.

In order to consider this, we must first consider the purpose of creating a new model of government in the first place. For the purposes of democratic government, a model is a representation of systems and processes designed to create a society that offers maximum benefit for all. Models help us explore political theories using simplified representations of a social reality in a defined environment. Hypotheses and experiments based on a model allow observers to predict the effects of employing the model, and yield meaningful data. Models are not designed to be stagnant, but to allow careful, calculated adjustments based on acquired data. Employed properly, these adjustments can foster continuous improvement. A common criticism of modeling has always been that it is highly mechanical in its nature and cannot incorporate the cultural relevance of communities. Fortunately, the advances made in adaptive modeling techniques have compensated for this inherent shortfall to a great degree.

The construction of government models is for the most part the purview of political scientists. Models should be designed so that their designers should be able to observe the result of an existing model and use those results to improve the model. Consequently, models are central to the process of gathering knowledge to build new governmental structures, with the hope of creating effective democracy across human society.

In the social sciences, this type of complex modeling is a unique analytical undertaking based on quantifying empirical information from different sources across the various fields, from psychology to economics, sociology to political science. Computers have long played a role in such analysis. Computer models make it possible to formulate complex theories about social processes, carry out experiments, and observe theoretical performance. One example of this is in economics, where computers can be used to analyze historical data, market trends, consumer psychology, and the impact of new regulations.

Political scientists have also benefitted from the use of computers to create and analyze models of government. But any models created must be based on a clear understanding of the causes of failure for existing and historical models.

The simple explanation for the failure of modern governments has been to simply blame the traditional communities for their social and cultural inaptitude, lack of civil society, and rule of law. However, the transformation of traditional societies to modernity requires a clear assessment of those societies by creating a model that analyzes social, cultural and political structures and furthermore the application and impact of these structures to contemporary social problems. It is important to remember that governments do not change overnight. The civil society and rule of law did not emerge immediately and in perfect form. It took over a hundred years to gradually transfer traditional governments to modern democratic ones.

The main thesis of this book is that Iran has historically prospered when its people have organized around a common set of ideas and principles that fostered diversity and local governance rather than around a highly centralized state that controlled all resources and suppressed diversity, and that a return to local governments that welcome a diversity of participants and ideas can bring prosperity back.

Hence, the goal of this book is not to present a complete or imposed model of governance but to open up discourse on the possibility of Iran and the other MENA nations taking a leadership role in shaping a new form of governance that transcends the endemic challenges of the modern state in the West.

CHAPTER ONE

Introduction to Iranian History
A New Interpretation [1]

A nation which does not remember what it was yesterday does not know what it is today.
We are trying to do a futile thing if we do not know where we came from or what we have been about.—Woodrow Wilson

Iran is arguably the oldest state in the world, but its past history is shrouded in the unknown, with many riddles and an enigmatic conclusion.

By the late nineteenth century, European scholars were beginning to discover Iranian antiquity and Iran's glorious history. At the time, Iranians knew little of this information; the nation was slowly waking up to modern life. Over 90 percent of the population, or about eleven million Iranians, lived in small rural villages. Most city dwellers remained illiterate. A very few people had some education, but no one was concerned about classical history. Mythology satisfied the curious, and analytical questions about history were rarely asked. The prevailing and abject poverty did not allow the luxury of such contemplation.

In the late nineteenth and early twentieth century, which was also the height of the Age of Imperialism, a new narrative based on a chauvinistic cultural consciousness emerged in Europe. Bloody wars over market shares aside, Europeans united in creating a newly minted concept that would be called European civilization. The best analogy to describe it is a flexible lens that Europeans could use to magnify the accomplishments of European peoples and diminish the accomplishments of others. By extension, this lens implied how others should see themselves. After World War I, the American economic ascent expanded the concept beyond Europe's borders. European civilization became known as Western civilization. Its basis is the idea that the classical Greek democracy and Plato's Academy in ancient Athens were linked directly with modern Europe, and that Greek rational thought and political organization were directly linked to the emergence of the modern democratic state.

In truth there is absolutely no direct link between the Athens academy and the Europe of the thirteenth to seventeenth century. This link was severed when the Emperor Justinian closed the school under pressure from Christians around 529 CE, the time that Europe plunged into the Dark Ages. In addition, modern democracies are based on individual freedoms, including the right of free speech. In classical Greece, the majority of people had no rights, and there was no guarantee of individual liberty. In fact, the Greek philosopher Socrates was put to death for expressing his views. What is presented as democracy was more like mob rule, and, in total, the Greek democratic state lasted less than sixty years.

The Western civilization narrative was developed based not on historical fact but on a chauvinistic and perhaps racist interpretation of history that bypasses and belittles the very important contribution of non-European civilizations to the development of the modern state. This narrative divided humanity, and this divisive approach to history has had an adverse political impact within the Western world and beyond.

The modern state's impact on the quality of life and on human consciousness is great. Perhaps it is humanity's greatest social achievement since the agricultural development of Neolithic times. But its creation is the culmination of all previous human experiences and developments. The Western civilization narrative by its nature denies the contribution of many other cultures and presents the development of modern culture as a linear one beginning and ending in Europe. This denial of the contributions of much of humanity has been Europe's justification for its barbaric actions toward colonized peoples.[2] And although the Imperial powers of Europe shared the concept of Western civilization, the Germans manufactured a new narrative of their own, which would later satisfy their nationalist and racial obsessions.

The Development of the Aryan Narrative

In early part of twentieth century, the Germans began to develop the idea that their culture was descended from Aryan "nobles" and was therefore a superior race. Later, using Hitler's twisted logic, this gave Germany license to cleanse humanity of people they deemed inferior. This narrative of Aryan supremacy had roots in the Persian Achaemenid dynasty of 600 BCE. But for the Germans, the historical connection was a propaganda tool, and their interpretation of Persian history had little to do with the actual facts. Iranians found the notion of racial superiority a totally alien concept, yet once introduced by the Germans, the concept found support.

The impact of this information on Iran was enormous. This traditional Middle Eastern nation had a rich, illustrious and colorful history. But by the early twentieth century, it had endured 800 years of desperate poverty. Further, many Iranians had little knowledge of their country's past glory. For hundreds of years, the majority had understood the nation's past and present condition via a mythical narrative without any precision, in which heroes fought for justice in support of the powerless. Sharia (Islamic jurisprudence) forbade objective academic research, so the nation's real history and its present condition remained hidden. Yet military events of the early nineteenth century had provided some degree of awakening, and national self-awareness had begun.

Crushed in the 1820s by Russia's modern military, Iranians had become painfully aware of their nation's weakness in comparison to the West. They began to understand slowly that the roots of that weakness lay in the nation's chronic sociopolitical and economic problems. Iran had lacked any institutions of higher learning for centuries, and the defeat by Russia clashed with Iran's mythical notions of its past. Still, the political system could not acknowledge or accept this, and it in fact became a personal problem for Iran's rulers.

Given these conditions, the new Aryan ideal proved very appealing. With its acceptance, notions of inadequacy could be assuaged. As with other racist ideologies, Aryanism offered justification for failure. It was much easier to blame others — in this case the Arabs — for Iran's condition than to accept responsibility. The Arabs became an easy target, as did Islam, which Iranians began to view as a religion brutally imposed on a noble nation by invading Arab armies.

This simplistic approach to complex historical events dominated the meager intellectual activity of Iran's elites. The first modern learning institution, the University of Tehran, was established in 1935, with the help of Germans. Initially, it did not emphasize research in social sciences and Persian literature and history.

The creation of Tehran University was just part of the drive for modernization that occurred under Reza Shah, the former prime minister who had eventually overthrown the Qajar dynasty. Since becoming Shah, he had taken steps to build the foundation of a modern Iranian state. These steps included convincing Russia to withdraw from Iran, undertaking large road-construction projects, and building the Trans-Iranian Railway.

The introduction of Marx and Marxism in Iran also occurred in the early twentieth century. Again, Eurocentrism played a role in the interpretation of Iranian history. The simplistic application of class theory advanced by Marx included a vague concept of the "Asiatic mode of production." Despite its weak foundation, this concept dominated the field, and Marxists showed little interest in studying the underlying conditions of Iranian society. They simply were not interested in details. Later, Marxists would argue that the underdevelopment of Iran was the result of capitalist exploitation of the nation's resources. They didn't attempt to better understand why historical events occurred, or to uncover the specifics of these events. Similar to the religious teachers of Iran's past, they presented their arguments with a self-righteous justification of simple truth that would be self-evident to "believers." Since the only social arguments in Iran for the past 800 years had been between believers and nonbelievers, this pattern of debate proved very acceptable.

In August of 1941, Iran was attacked by Britain and Russia, which viewed Reza Shah as a possible German ally and needed Iranian territory for the transport of war materials. The relative peace and security that Iran had enjoyed for the previous fifteen years came to an abrupt end, as did the modernizing efforts of Reza Shah. Over the next twenty-two years, Iran witnessed numerous political upheavals, which culminated in the consolidation of power by Mohammad Reza Shah in 1963. Another period of political stability opened the way for efforts to change Iran's basic socioeconomic conditions.

At the end of this period, the Islamists rose to power, in part by presenting a revised viewpoint on the historical Islamization of Iran. These Islamists argued that Iranians had welcomed the Arab invaders of the seventh century, and had accepted Islam with open arms as salvation from the corrupt shahs of the past. The rise to power of the Islamists in Iran was aided by the popularization of Marxist sentiments held by the elites. The powerful combination of Islamist and Marxist ideology expressed itself in the 1979 revolution that overthrew the shah. Among the revolution's goals were to eliminate all Western imperialist influences, return Iran to its Islamic roots, and return the nation to social, economic, and cultural glory.

From the Constitutional Revolution of 1906, which had established the nation's first parliament, until today, Iran has only enjoyed twenty-five years of peace and stability. During this brief period, higher education understandably focused on educating the doctors and engineers necessary for modernization. The project of understanding 2500 years of Iranian history requires a multidisciplinary, institutional approach only possible in a sustained period of prosperity and security. Because of this, it has remained mostly the pursuit of individuals, not institutions.

As such, the following analysis represents a small yet significant step to approaching Iranian history through an Iranian viewpoint, rather than through Western civilization's lens of Eurocentrism or Orientalism that has dominated the study of history.

The Emergence of Iran — Cyrus the Great and Darius the Great, the Founding Fathers

The emergence of Iran as a state has always been a puzzle to historians. Its rapid development altered the fundamentals of the existing political order and the course of human development. Cyrus the Great created what is today the State of Iran during his reign in the sixth century BCE. We can safely claim that from its inception, Iran was just an idea, one Cyrus the Great conceived by observing the existing sociopolitical structures of his world. His ideas about the political structure of the state were categorically different from that of contemporary states, and of those ideas that had come before.

What Cyrus began and Darius the Great later completed was a new approach to state and governmental structure and function. For the first time, the principles of cooperation and the encouragement of trade became primary political factors. This sharply contrasted with the previous political order established by Assyria, which preceded Cyrus.

Starting as early as the twenty-fifth century BCE, Assyria built the most efficient military state the world had ever seen. The army was at the heart of state organization, and the state was built around a standing army. The principal business of the nation had been war; its wealth and prosperity were sustained by booty and by the extraction of resources from other supervised populations. A military bureaucracy carried out the functions of government at home and in conquered regions, establishing the first centralized imperial control over vast provincial territories.

The defeat of the Israeli Kingdom in 721 BCE was just one example of Assyria's brutal system of conquest and occupation. After a period of looting and massacre, Assyria deported the remainder of the healthy Israeli population to western parts of today's Iran. This marked the original disappearance of the Ten Tribes of Israel.

Assyria's approach to the religious beliefs of the people it conquered was similarly destructive. The Assyrian king described himself as a son of God. He challenged other theologies by imposing his religion on those he conquered and deporting his vanquished foes' religious leaders.

The Assyrian empire eventually fell victim to military attack and by 609 BCE no longer existed. But its successors, the Neo-Babylonians, continued the Assyrian pattern of government. In 597 the Neo-Babylonian empire defeated the Kingdom of Judah and sent its population to Babylon in captivity. This militaristic sociopolitical pattern of government was a reflection of this period's human consciousness and the accepted order of state and political governance.

Cyrus's genius was to recognize the futility of this order and to imagine and implement an alternative governmental pattern that benefited the development of humanity. Cyrus's new political order was based essentially on cooperation among nations, respect for established cultural and religious practices and national identity, and a strong emphasis on the promotion of commerce among conquered foes.

Friends and foes alike recognized Cyrus for his self-control, honesty, kindness, strength, and pursuit of justice. These characteristics helped make Cyrus the transformative figure of his time — and helped make the ascent of Persia possible. Before Cyrus, Persia was a small nation far from the main centers of the power. Yet in part because of Cyrus's moral authority, the forces sent to battle against him instead converted to his ideas and merged with him.

Later, his treatment of Pantia, a beautiful wife of an Armenian general, won him Armenian support and forged an alliance. The gentle treatment of defeated Croesus, King of Lydia, forged a life-long friendship. One can speculate that Cyrus's ability to articulate a better future for those who believed in him played a role in his success. Today, Europeans view him as a successful general similar to Julius Caesar. In contrast, the Bible's Old Testament refers to him as a prophet. Perhaps Cyrus the Great was more like Moses than Caesar. After all, he is the one who conceived the idea of Iran.

After his ascension to power in 522 BCE, the Persian king Darius the Great institutionalized Cyrus's moral and organizational code into the largest empire that has ever existed. Darius united the ancient civilizations of the Indus, Euphrates, and Nile valleys for the first time under a single political administration that believed in the preservation of national identity and strongly promoted commerce and interaction among these civilizations. Darius's works included the building of numerous roads and canals and the creation of a system of universal currency. Together, these works helped facilitate an amazing period of human interaction and exchange of ideas. It was not the military might of Persia that dominated the ancient world. Rather, it was the concept of creating a better life through harmony and coexistence. In fact, fewer than one million Persians eventually controlled an empire that included more than thirty million subjects. This transformative time changed the course of human development.

Darius placed an inscription on his tomb that was likely meant for those who would follow him to the throne. He revealed himself to be mortal, not divine, an admission his predecessors had never made; in fact he considers himself to be a friend of his fellow humans. Darius further advised his successors to be honest, to deal justly with both the powerful and the powerless, to guard against deceit, and to live in moderation, with an emphasis on self-control. He further advised Persians to be good gardeners and to bring order to the chaos of the wild environment.

Darius had employed such values to bring peace and prosperity and to create the largest empire in the world. The Persian empire connected three distinct human civilizations under a unified political system that allowed for differences while promoting economic growth thorough the exchange of new commodities. From the Indus Valley, rice and fowl found their way to other parts of the empire. The

Nile Valley added sugar and other agricultural products, and from Iran came various foods from its fruit trees. The economic prosperity also enriched other trade partners, including Greece. These changes set humanity on the course of coexistence and influenced all the political systems that followed.

Iran was founded to use political position not to force culture on subjugated peoples, but as a platform for human coexistence. The principles established by Cyrus and implemented by Darius became the three pillars of Iranian identity:

1. Self-control (Humility)
2. Truthfulness (Justice)
3. Protection of the less powerful (Community)

The pillars of Iranian identity have manifested themselves throughout the nation's long history in different forms and organizations. They have influenced the political order and are foundational to religious thought and practices. In short, Iran is the embodiment of these values.

These values must have been embodied in Darius's meeting in Persepolis with sovereign national leaders each year on Narwuz, the Persian New Year. The meeting must have taken place in the Hall of Nations. Xerxes later built gates to this hall that are known as Xerxes's Gate of All Nations. Persepolis was free from the depictions of vanquished people in pain, which had been the norm.

Gradually, the passage of time eroded the institutions Darius had created. The powerful became more self-indulgent. The moral values that had controlled the powerful and protected the powerless eroded into instruments of repression. The humility and self-control of rulers moved from the realm of temporal political power and institutions into mythical heroic fictions. The institutions of power became mere instruments of social control as the powerful created social castes and became more interested in class privilege and the accumulation of power and wealth for themselves. For the powerless, protection existed only in the mythical domain. It seemed as if the inscriptions on Darius's tomb had been totally forgotten.

The Sasanian Dynasty

Over seven hundred years later, Shapur I, who considered himself to be a rightful descendant of Cyrus the Great, became king of the Sasanian empire in Iran. His reign typified that of Sasanian kings, and showed how far removed from Cyrus's principles Persian leaders had become. According to legend, after capturing Roman Emperor Valerian, Shapur used the defeated man as a step stool for mounting his horse and ordered depictions of the humiliating scene carved on a mountainside for all to see near the Tomb of Darius.

The Sasanians ruled Persia for more than four centuries. Their most lasting achievement was the creation of a caste-based sociopolitical order that denied mobility to its citizens. The social upheavals of the Mazdakite revolution of the fifth and sixth centuries forced the institutional reforms of the Sasanian king, Khosrow Anoushiravan.

In the end, however, the aspirations of the population for social change were suppressed. The caste system was reinforced and a new class of farmland owners was added. The political administrations were revised by dividing the country into four semiautonomous regions. The autonomous eastern province of Khorason with its vibrant economy enjoyed a more relaxed social structure and it became the supporter of the rebellion of Bahrum Chobin's civil war of

590 CE against the rule of the Sasanian Dynasty. However, else-where the reforms further concentrated the king's power, creating even more opportunity for self-indulgence.

The harsh nature of caste stratification is embodied in a story by Ferdosi, the Iranian historian/poet of the tenth century. In the story, Khosrow Anoushiravan needed money for a campaign against Rome. A shoemaker was willing to offer any sum that Anoushiravan needed if the shoemaker's son could receive an education that was reserved for a higher caste. As commoners were not allowed to be educated, Anoushiravan declined the shoemaker's offer. Such was the condition of Iran under the Sasanian kings.

The decadence of Sasanians reached a new height with Khosrow Parviz, who expanded the territories of the empire by invading Jeru-salem and Egypt. However, his immoral personal behavior set up a chain of events that eventually turned the triumph into a disastrous defeat. On the way to conquer Jerusalem, Parviz passed through Hira, a Sasanian vassal state. Its ruler was Naemon, of the Lakhmid dynasty. Parviz, who had heard of the beauty of Naemon's daughter, ordered the vassal to bring her to him. Naemon refused and took his daughter and his wealth to his Arab foes, the Shybani tribes of northern Arabia, for safekeeping.[3]

When Naemon returned, Parviz had him immediately put to death and annexed Hira to be administered under direct Persian rule. After two decades, this chain of events led to the invasion of Iran by the Arabs. At this point, it is valuable to contrast the lust of Parviz, who kept more than 1000 women in his harem, with the self-control of Cyrus, who behaved honorably toward Pantia, the beautiful wife of an Armenian general, and created a productive, long-lasting alliance with Armenia.

After the conquest of Jerusalem, during which he damaged the

Church of the Holy Sepulchre and captured and removed the True Cross, Khosrow Parviz wrote a letter to Heraclius insulting Christ and Christians. When Parviz's letter reached Constantinople the city was under siege by the Persian general Shahrbaraz.

The Persians stood at the very gates of Constantinople, and Heraclius had prepared to abandon the city and move the capital to his native Carthage in North Africa. With the arrival of Khosrow Parviz's letter, the powerful church patriarch Sergius, convinced that Christianity was in danger, melted all the church's gold and gave it to Heraclius in return for a defense of the city.

Heraclius used the gold to rebuild his military forces. He sailed to Armenia, whose people were also aggravated by Khosrow's insult on their religion and culture. Heraclius rapidly defeated a mighty Persian army and later attacked Iran along the Tigris River. He nearly captured Ctesiphon, the imperial capital. Heraclius won peace after a coup in 628 CE in which Kavadh II killed his father Khosrow Parviz. Parviz's lust, arrogance, and greed had turned an assured victory into a major defeat for Iran.

The Evolution of Islam

The same year that Parviz died, a confederacy of Meccan forces besieged Medina, held by Muslims under Muhammad. The Muslims built a trench to defend against the Meccans' horse and camel cavalry. The siege failed, and the Meccan confederacy disintegrated.

In contrast, the Muslims cooperation pact known as the Charter of Medina created the Ummah alliance, the most financially rewarding and strongest political entity in Arabia. In 630 CE, Muslim forces took the city of Mecca without a fight, and treated the conquered Meccan people respectfully. But in 631CE, Muhammad ordered all members of the Ummah alliance to convert to Islam. In 632 CE, before this could happen, Muhammad died. His passing started a revolt against Muslims across the Arabian Peninsula known as the Ridda Wars. The wars represented a massive defection from the Ummah alliance.

Only Medina, Mecca, and Taif remained loyal to the Ummah alliance. However, because of the disunity of the opposition, Medina remained the strongest force. Muhammad's successor, Caliph Abu Bakr, took decisive action to crush the rebellion. But it was just matter of the time before other alliances would challenge Medina's power. Muhammad's last military expedition of Tabuk against Rome did not justify the cost of mobilization of about thirty thousand troops and had remained inconclusive at the time of Muhammad's death. The survival of Islam depended on finding a way that the alliance could provide for the tribes who had stayed loyal to Ummah. This could have been the end of Ummah and possibly Islam if new resources were not found. The Ummah war with Rome had stagnated, and it was not producing enough momentum to satisfy the financial needs of the members.

Around this time Al-Muthanna ibn Harithah of the Arab Shybani tribe (the same person to whom Naemon had entrusted his daughter and wealth for safekeeping) came to Medina to meet with Caliph Abu Bakr. He brought considerable gifts and informed Abu Bakr that his tribe had been successfully raiding southern Iranian territories for 15 years without any major obstacles. Muthanna ibn Harithah knew that he needed additional military support to raid deeper into Iranian territory. He said he would be willing to accept Islam and pay a quarter of all his captured treasure to Abu Bakr in return for protection.

Abu Bakr realized that this was the solution to all his problems. The financially rewarding alliance united the tribes and eliminated all the threats to the Ummah alliance. Abu Bakr appointed Khalid ibn al-Walid as the leader of a mostly volunteer Muslim army. The campaign began with small raids into southern Iran (what is now southern Iraq). Abu Bakr started small because the Arab soldiers under his command tended to fear Persians with a deep conviction. This fear ran in the Arab tribal consciousness as a racial complex; perhaps it was the result of centuries of Persian power and glory. In return, the Persians regarded the Arabs of southern Arabia with contempt as too poor and uncivilized to annex to their empire. Abu Bakr understood that if his Arab soldiers suffered any defeat at the hand of the Persians, it would justify their fear.

After entering Iraq with his army of 18,000, Khalid won decisive victories in four consecutive battles: the Battle of Chains, fought in April 633 CE; the Battle of River, fought in the 3rd week of April 633 CE; the Battle of Walaja, fought in May 633 CE, and the Battle of Ullais, fought in late May, 633 CE. After twenty years of Khosrow Parviz's futile wars and Parviz's murder of seasoned generals, the Persian army had lost its strength and organization. Finally, less than twenty years after the death of Parviz, the Sasanian dynasty came to a bitter end at the battle of Nahavand in 642 CE, opening a new chapter for the majority of Iranians.

In summary, less than one year from the revolt of Ridda, in which a majority in the Arabian peninsula left Islam and fought against Islam and Medina rule, a ragtag tribal army of Muslims achieved a major upset, and the Sasanian dynasty fell.

It is important to consider, however, that the Islamic identity of the Arab warriors fighting under Abu Bakr is highly questionable. Five years was not enough time to change many centuries of social habits and behaviors. The warriors were not religious zealots, and they had no concept of participating in what today we might call a "mission from god" to convert the Iranian people.

What is certain is that the promise of the spoils of war and the opportunity to improve their living conditions drove the Arabs to join the army and fight. The wars provided a better future for the survivors and forward motion to keep Islamic rule from disintegration. Certainly Khosrow Parviz's futile twenty years' war had exhausted both Persia and Rome, and his immoral behavior and miscalculation had opened the door to Arab armies.

The battle of Nahavand in 642 CE effectively brought Sasanian rule to an end. By and large, Arabs did not change the political structure of the communities they ruled. Locally, the same people who had been in power for centuries remained in power. The choice of whether to cooperate or to revolt was decided by traditional rulers, with very little input from lower-caste people. Many municipalities and local rulers cooperated with the Arabs. Some converted to Islam to be considered as part of the Ummah alliance and to receive part of the war spoils and tax money generated by invasion and occupation. Others joined the Arab armies to fight for a larger share of war spoils. But most local rulers and citizens accepted the realities of occupation. The notable exception was Khorason which resulted in some setbacks for Arabs. Qutayba ibn Muslim from 705 to 715 CE committed many atrocities against the population in order to bring this region under Arab control; however after his death in 715 CE until the revolt of Abu Muslim the region was for the most part free from Arabs. In other regions paying taxes to the Arab occupiers gave Iranians the freedom to live their lives based on their own social traditions, customs, and values. In most instances the taxes paid to the Arabs were lower than Sasanian taxes had been.

This coexistence continued for many generations of Iranians, who grew up and lived in societies that were for the most part isolated, fragmented farming communities. Perhaps very infrequently, tax collectors came to collect their due. The caste system remained firmly in place, social mobility and social change remained impossible, and, for most people, life continued as it had for centuries.

The Islamification of Iran

In 634 CE, as he lay dying, Abu Bakr named Umar ibn al-Khattab, who had been a companion of Muhammad, as his successor. Umar soon realized that if he allowed the coexistence of Iranians and Arabs to continue, the Islamic identity of the Arab soldiers would disappear. To prevent this, he built two new cities, Kufa and Basra, to garrison his soldiers. The Arabs built many more of these garrison towns; Shiraz, a small village about a day's travel from the Iranian City of Estakhr, a provincial capital of the Sasanian empire, became the garrison city for the Fars province in 693 CE after numerous unsuccessful uprisings against the Arab invaders.

To create garrisons, Umar chose locations about one day's journey from many of Iran's urban areas. This meant the soldiers would be close enough to prevent any uprising but not so close as to encourage significant cultural mingling.

The decision to build garrison towns after the invasion of Iran was likely based on military need. In a short period of time, the Muslims had become rulers of a very vast territory. The Prophet Muhammad had died, and his charismatic influence was gone. But by providing economic rewards to their soldiers, and by attacking a wealthy but dysfunctional empire, the Arabs had succeeded beyond their wildest dreams.

Still, all would have been lost if the invaders had merged with the local populations. Clearly the locals would have been much more sophisticated urbanites, and the allure of city life would likely have proven irresistible. It would have been just a matter of time before the invaders would have disappeared into the fabric of the existing society. The fragile Islamic leadership would have melted away.

Garrison life provided a critical social structure that prevented this from happening. Arab society and social structures were tribal: tribal identity superseded any other loyalties. In garrison towns, young recruits were incorporated into a fighting force under the leadership of a trusted Arab tribe with a familiar structure and customs. At the same time, these soldiers forged new Islamic identities. Arab armies often included Iranian military units defeated in battle, whose soldiers also wanted to improve their prospects through war. They, too, became part of life in garrison towns, and also became Islamicized.

The decision to keep the Arab invaders separate from the Iranian population was an ingenious solution to the problems at hand. The socialization and training of individuals with such a hunger for adventure and wealth could only take place in a closed community created by the garrison towns. In Iran's larger urban areas, such tasks would have been impossible. However, the consequences of this decision would be much greater than Arab leaders could imagine. It would lead to the development of vibrant Islamic communities in Iran.

Plato's Academy in Exile

On the eve of a critical battle in 312 CE, Emperor Constantine of Rome claimed to have had a vision of Christian imagery promising victory. Under the banner of Christianity, his troops fought and won the battle, eventually taking control of the Roman empire and legalizing the Christian religion. By then, the Roman empire had split, with the Western Roman empire seated at Rome and the Eastern Roman or Byzantine empire seated at Constantinople.

The Western Roman empire had already begun a rapid decline. Between 300 CE and 700 CE in Europe, the Migration Period, also called the Barbarian Invasions, was a period of human migration marking the transition from Late Antiquity to the Early Middle Ages. These movements were catalyzed by profound changes, political instability, and social upheaval across nearly the entire European continent. Europe was known as the "barbarian frontier," owing to the military conflicts prompted by the migration of Goths, Vandals, Bulgars, Alans, Suebi, Frisians, and Franks, among other Germanic, Iranian, and Slavic tribes from central Asia and eastern Europe. During this period, Rome was sacked a number of times. Its sacking by Germanic forces in 476 CE is held by many historians to mark the effective end of the Western Roman empire.

In the Eastern Roman empire following the legalization of Christianity, Roman and pagan tolerance of religious and cultural diversity evolved into a unified Christian state religion with very little tolerance for other beliefs or social institutions. In 391 CE, Emperor Theodosius I outlawed paganism. That same year, the patriarch of Alexandria closed the pagan temples and the Library of Alexandria.

The state's religious zealotry could not tolerate the existence of Plato's Academy in Athens. Off and on, it had existed for over a thousand years, teaching philosophy and other disciplines. In 529 CE, the emperor Justinian closed the school. The last scholars of the Academy, including Damascius, traveled to Ctesiphon in Iran to seek the protection of Sasanian king Khosrow Anoushiravan. After the *pax perpetua,* a peace treaty of 532 between Persia and the Byzantine empire, Athenian scholars were banned from teaching. But their personal security and tolerance for their beliefs were ensured. They were forbidden to return to Athens but were allowed to live in places such as Harran, located in northern Mesopotamia, which is today southern Turkey.

Overall, there was a vast difference in the social and political structure of traditional Iranian towns, Roman Christian towns, and Islamic garrison towns. Traditional Iranian society was dominated by a rigid caste structure. The artisans and traders belonged to lower social castes, and their wealth and possessions did not change their social standing in the community. The Christian societies of the Roman empire suffered from a similar fate. Intolerant, often corrupt rulers of the Church would not allow the freedom to change.

Yet without social change and mobility, any society will stagnate. Economic, political, and cultural growth all depend upon the ability of individuals to exercise creativity and experience personal growth. The growth of individuals is a function of a society's tolerance for personal liberty, its access to education, and its support for change.

These points are best illustrated in the Diffusion of Innovations Curve, or Rogers Curve. It implies that in any society, about 2.5 percent of people have a desire to change their living conditions and are perhaps looking for a different life. These people innovate and create new possibilities for change. This group is followed by a group that represents about 13.5 percent of society. The significance of this second group is that they are the early adopters, or followers of the first group. The next two segments are the 34 percent of the population that will gradually change and the 16 percent that will never change. These percentages, with some adjustments, are constant in any human society, past, present, or future. In fact, the difference in social progress and economic development of any society is directly related to the ability of these individual innovators to function and grow with the support of their communities.

The caste system of the Sasanian empire and the religious zealotry of the Romans prevented individual growth, innovation, and social change. However, the newly formed garrison towns of the Arabs had unique and interesting characteristics. Their population was a mix of young individuals usually gathered from different tribes. They had joined the movement in search of adventure or because they wanted to better their lives. They had accepted Islam, but Islam at this time had no clergy and no defined religious jurisprudence, or *fiqh* (the Arabic equivalent).

Tax collection was the main business of garrison soldiers. They had access to all the excess financial resources of any area — something the military machine needed to survive, as military campaigns consume everything that an economy can produce. Armies need housing, food, and military hardware. They need trade workers to prepare and build weapons, clothing, and fortifications. As such, the garrison towns must have been magnets for economic activity.

The prevailing social order within these small towns must have been very interesting as well. Islam was a new idea; struggle against the tribes of Arabia was the path. Or perhaps the personal interpretation of their deeds mixed with tribal customs governed the behavior of these towns. The residents of garrison towns had enough latitude to decide for themselves based on tribal customs and basic Islamic values as they understood them at the time. The only valid guide that was universally respected was Muhammad's way of living his life. This practice of Islam became known as Sunnite, or Sunni.

Life in garrison towns echoed that of all frontier towns. People lived using a combination of the tools, ideas, and social structures they brought with them and those obtained locally. This life must have been difficult in the beginning. Arabs had never been an imperial power, and they knew little of this Persian land they now controlled. Prior to their arrival, their knowledge was likely limited to the tales of merchants and contacts with Persians in Yemen and the few Persians who lived with Muslims. The social structures of Persia seemed unfamiliar, too. Muslim tribal social structures are very egalitarian, with no distinct ranking within the tribe.

In Iran, established farming communities had lived without much mobility and with the same stagnating Sasanian caste system for many centuries. Sasanian leadership introduced a new class of dehghan, a caste of rural aristocracy, but things remained much the same. Numerous peasant revolts had been brutally suppressed by military force. The garrison towns offered new opportunities to artisans and tradespeople struggling against the limits of their castes. In garrison towns, where the egalitarian structure of tribal society dominated, castes went largely unrecognized. There, lower-caste people had the opportunity to earn more money and achieve higher status.

Eventually, these Iranians became part of the social fabric of the garrison towns. Most of the Arabs in the garrisons had come from one tribe and been adopted by another. Perhaps it is safe to assume that the adoption of a new group of Iranian tradespeople and artisans must have followed the same pattern of socialization. Other groups of social outcasts, including exiled members of Plato's Academy and those persecuted by the Church, also found their way to garrison towns.

Arabs followed the same pattern of building for all garrison towns, which were built behind advancing Arab armies. This structure provided many opportunities for economic growth.

Trade and mercantilism were the main commercial activities in which Arabs had historically engaged. So trade started between these new garrison communities, and their economic prosperity attracted more and more people. Artisans and tradespeople who had lived humble lives in the old caste systems became wealthy and respected merchants in Islamic garrison towns.

With the passing of a hundred years, the garrison towns went from novelty to a permanent part of the new Iranian landscape. By the time of the Abu Muslim revolution in 747 CE, several generations of Iranians had lived all of their lives in these towns. The political and social organization of these towns remained more or less the same, but the majority of the population was of Iranian origin. This writer estimates that migrants to these towns represented less than 15 percent of the population.

Hasan of Basra

One way to illustrate these social changes would be to follow the life of Hasan of Basra (642-728), a person who lived in these times. Our information from this period comes from many written sources and can be independently verified.

The effort to gain economic advantage has motivated most human endeavors. If we follow Hasan of Basra's life we can witness a pattern of possible social changes that took place in Islamic garrison towns and how the Islamic community empowered those who sought a better life for themselves.

Hasan was born in 642 CE, the same year as the Battle of Nahavand, which ended Sasanian rule. He lived to the year 728 CE, or about 86 years. His father, Pirouz, was a low-caste Iranian captured perhaps before the Battle of Ghadesieh and brought to Medina as slave. Later, Pirouz converted to Islam and was freed. He married

Khara, and Hasan was born in Medina. In 657 CE, at the age of 15, Hasan moved to Basra, a garrison town.

As a young man, Hasan took part in the conquests and campaigns in eastern Iran. Later, he returned to Basra and became a jewel merchant known as Hasan of the Pearls. Hasan often traveled to Rome for trade; it is possible that he became familiar with the teachings of the then-defunct Plato's Academy. In any case, he managed to educate himself. Later in his life, Hasan became a teacher in Basra and founded a school. He became famous for his teachings about human choice and free will, and he attracted many students, including Amr ibn Ubayd (d.761) and Wasil ibn Ata (d.749), the founders of Mu'tazilah, of which we will soon learn more.

Hasan's experience exemplifies that of many other Iranians in garrison towns. The son of a slave, he left home at age 15 to follow his destiny and seek his fortune. After a few years of expedition and conquest in eastern Iran he returned to Basra and used his perhaps modest fortune to become a wealthy merchant. In the process, he was able to educate himself. He became a teacher and opened a school to teach others. This story shows not only the possibility for personal advancement in garrison towns, but also how such advancement could contribute enormous benefits to society. Hasan's personal achievements were only possible because the society that he lived in had empowered him, enabled him, and provided him with the free will to follow his dream.

Iranian garrison towns of the seventh and early eighth centuries were in most part similar to the frontier towns of the American West. Very little social order existed, the new religion had not yet developed institutions of power, and residents enjoyed a great deal of personal and social freedom. Hasan's life in Basra was not an exception but in fact the rule. Numerous Iranians migrated to these cities to be free of the caste system and in search of fulfillment, and found it. In comparison, social mobility and similar freedoms could not have been possible for the citizens of a traditional Iranian town. In fact, most Iranians remained in their caste and did not travel perhaps more than a few miles from their homes in their entire lives.

It was among the people of Basra that a new school of Islam arose: Mu'tazilah. Its tenets included a rational approach to observation of the social and natural world and empowered individual decision-making based on reason. It was the modern lifestyle of its time.

The theology of the Mu'tazilah school allowed followers to apply the process of *kalam,* or reaching a unique conclusion through debate and argument, to their understanding of the Koran. They argued that because of God's perfection and the eternal nature of it, the Koran could not be co-eternal with God. Therefore, the Koran must have been created. Based on this premise, the Mu'tazilah school reasoned that the injunctions or demands of God are attainable by rational thought and rational inquiry, since knowledge is derived from reason. Therefore, reason is the "final arbiter" in distinguishing right from wrong.

This powerful concept implied that man's reasoning was in some way equivalent to God's injunctions. And it follows, in Mu'tazilah reasoning, that "sacred precedent" is not an effective means of determining what is just. What is obligatory in religion is only obligatory "by virtue of reason."

The influence of Greek philosophy and other teachings and the research methods of Plato's Academy are prevalently detectable in Mu'tazilah reasoning. It is possible that the influence was relatively direct. The simple fact is that the economic success of garrison towns attracted many wanderers. And we know that since the closure of the Academy about a century before, exiles from the school had been looking for a home free from religious dogmas. It is very likely that many exiles from the Academy may have migrated to garrison towns, where their teaching could have influenced several generations.

The social impact on Iran of these fast-growing towns, which offered social mobility to their citizens and a rational approach to solving human problems, must have been great — even in the larger traditional communities. The rate of transformation must have been slow, but with the passing of a hundred years, the realities of social mobility and the story of elevation of slaves to high social positions must have traveled to all parts of the country and collided with the traditional social structure, which in the past had been enforced by Sasanian imperial military forces.

As time passed, the links between garrison town residents and tribes in Arabia also weakened. Tribal social organization was becoming obsolete, with a growing non-Arab population gaining power. Eventually, revolution put an end to tribal organization and institutionalized a new political structure for these societies.

Behzadan pour Vandad Hormozd aka Abu Muslim Abd Rahman ibn Muslim Khorasani was born in 727 CE. He became the leader of a rebellion in Khorasan against the ruling Umayyad caliphate.

Like Hasan of Basra, Abu Muslim spent his early youth bound in slavery. He belonged to one of the secret organizations that supported the Abbasid clan. In 747, Abu Muslim was sent to the Marv oasis to lead the uprising being planned there against the ruling Umayyad Caliphate. He drew Iranian peasants, some Arab tribes, fugitive slaves, and some Dehghans (Land owners) into the uprising. From December 747 to January 748 the troops of the Abbasid clan, led by Abu Muslim, overran Marv. In 748 they took Nishapur and Tus (near present-day Masshad), and in 749 they defeated the

Umayyads near Nahavand. By early 750 they had achieved a decisive victory on the Great Zab River, and the Umayyad Caliphate fell. Any Arab tribesmen with any affiliation with Umayyad were either killed or escaped from Iran.

After the Abbasid clan came to power, Abu Muslim remained the deputy overlord in Khorasan. His heroic role in the revolution and his military skill, along with his conciliatory politics toward Shia, Sunnis, Zoroastrians, Jews, and Christians, made him extremely popular among the people. Abu Muslim was murdered on the orders of Caliph al-Mansur, who feared the growing influence of Abu Muslim and his popularity among non-Arabs. Still, the Abbasid Caliphate remained in power.

With the advent of Abu Muslim, for the first time an ordinary Iranian not related to any ruling castes was able to defeat and change the government. The tribes of central Arabia and tribal political customs ended. The impact of these and other social upheavals encouraged many communities to imagine and demand a different social order for themselves. This was the dawn of a new era. I believe that, at this point in history, fewer than 15 percent of Iranians had converted to Islam.

Conversion to Islamic Identity

The period from 750 CE to 850 CE is perhaps the most interesting in Iranian history. It featured a steep, widespread rise in the number of cults ruled by local prophets or community leaders who organized to demand social change. These demands were driven by the economic success of garrison towns and the political vacuum created by the fall of Sasanian dynastic rule. Among these were the various orders of darvishes, which were loose groups of agnostic (meaning non-Muslim) Iranians. The history of darvishes in Iran is very murky; we don't have any historical sources. However, we are aware of their existence. The similarity between darvish and Darius the Great, the old Persian pronunciation of his name, Darayavahush, is hard to ignore. It is highly probable that darvish orders were initially the incognito eyes and ears of the great king, traveling throughout the empire as the state intelligence organization, which later metamorphosed into various darvish orders. But these local darvish orders became more active in this period. The arrival of many defeated elements of Arab civil wars — first the Khavarej and later the Ali's Shia, who sought safe haven away from centers of political power — also played a role. These refugees penetrated many isolated rural communities of Iran as preachers of their own faith. Rural Iranian communities with a long history of bottled-up frustration and demand for social change and social equality were easy targets for conversion. These preachers, who in time became political leaders, reformulated the core Iranian values expressed by Cyrus the Great (Humility, Justice, and Community) and institutionalized by Darius. Remnants of these institutions or possibly local darvish orders were converted to Islam and later were identified as Islamic Sufis.

From 750 CE to 850 CE, most urban communities in Iran abandoned the social caste system of the Sasanian era and converted to a form of Islamic identity based on the pillars of Iranian identity, and expressed in a fashion unique to each community. By 850 CE, it is possible that more than half of Iran's population had converted to "Islam." However, mass adherence to a single interpretation of Islam did not occur.

At about the same time, a systematic migration of the traditional Zoroastrian communities to Gujarat in northern India began. The migration, which lasted for many centuries, reflected the social change taking place as the conversion to various orders of Islamic religion accelerated. Groups like the Zoroastrians, who wanted to uphold the traditional Sasanian social order, may have vigorously defended their way of life. But it was a hopeless battle.

The period from 850 CE to 1050 CE represents a truly amazing mixture of religious coexistence and community self-rule. The office of a ruling caliph created a "state" structure under a loosely defined Islamic banner. Some Islamic communities that grew out of garrison towns of earlier times had organic links to the office of the caliph. Increasingly, these connections became economic rather than political. There were many schools of *fiqh* (Islamic jurisprudence) being developed in this period. However, the power of the schools seldom reached beyond the urban hub in which they arose. Each hub was a center of economic activity for many smaller communities with totally diverse religious beliefs. Many of these smaller communities had enjoyed self-rule with very little input from their urban centers. However, economically both hub cities and smaller communities became part of the greater Islamic state. And in time many of these hubs were ruled by political strongmen.

In the early part of the Abbasid caliphate, the caliph appointed these urban rulers, who had a stronger link with the center. Gradually these links became more symbolic. Sharing part of collected taxes in the beginning later became occasional gifts for the office of caliph when communities needed an edict in their favor.

Even later, the strongmen were replaced with militant tribal leaders who assumed the role of the protectors of society. Power became concentrated in individual tribes, which later created local dynastic rulers. But the nature of the political order — local political sovereignty and economic integration with other communities — remained the same.

If we look at the state order at around the midpoint of this period, the Buyid, who controlled Baghdad, are the dominant power. The Buyid changed the caliphate at will, but they were very respectful of the office of the caliphate. The institution of the caliphate at the time of Muhammad was very strong, as the caliph manifested political, military, and religious authority. Buyid rulers used the old Sasanian titles, calling themselves Shahanshah. Although religiously they were Shia themselves, they saw value in keeping the caliph's office intact and never demolished it.

At the same time, many different local rulers paid nominal homage to the office of the caliph. They would occasionally send some gift to the caliph in support of a certain demand and perhaps for the sake of solidarity.

The power to abolish the Abbasid Islamic caliphate existed for many centuries, but the powerful always sought to preserve the existing arrangement of political structure and its economic links — and for good reason. Mercantilism was the source of prosperity and wealth. Rulers were very much aware of the economic importance of the system. The power relationship of the era is unique, but it is hard to conceive of any other form of government that could have preserved the existing economic networks and the social order.

Max Weber defines the state as the monopolizer of the violence. Using this definition, then, the Abbasid Caliphate cannot be considered a state. From the beginning, the Abbasid caliphs did not organize their own military forces. In fact, the social structure at the time was not conducive to such an idea. Instead, they relied on strongmen to maintain the political order in the empire. The form was actually very similar to Umayyads' tribal network, but since tribal connections had weakened, the political order was soon modified, and the Abbasid caliphs steadily lost power to the local leaders.

Eventually the caliph became a political figurehead in the hands of strongmen. The office of the caliph became a cheap source of political legitimacy, much like symbolic heads of state in modern times.

As time passed, the mighty old cities of Ctesiphon and Estakhr rapidly lost population, and the garrison towns grew. The new social order was based on trade and commercial activity, as the expansion of garrison town economies attracted more migrants. A rational approach to observations of nature and the possibility of social mobility was the order of these societies. Mu'tazilah beliefs dominated the social discourse. These included:

1. God is a distant God (i.e., man is in charge of his life).
2. The Koran was created.
3. *Vaieh*, or revelation, was rational deduction of human mind.

These beliefs are very close to those of modernity. The ability to learn became accessible to almost anyone in these hub cities, regardless of social background. An explosion of learning and invention rapidly spread across trade networks.

The accumulation of wealth, along with the desire to know more, allowed the establishment of many centers of learning with refined cultural activities and a rational approach to the observation of nature. Perhaps the influence of exiles from Plato's Academy played a role. In any case, these activities were being defined as Islamic. A Muslim of this period was part of a minority of people who defined themselves by a rational approach to learning similar to that practiced in Plato's Academy. Usually, these Muslims were free of many of the superstitions of the less-educated masses.

In the larger areas of countryside surrounding these urban hubs, a different form of development took shape. Local leaders adopted and championed the three principles of the Iranian identity that Cyrus and Darius had created:

1. Self-control (Humility)
2. Truthfulness, (Justice)
3. Protection of the less powerful (Community)

The community expression of these principles usually took the form of mystical, hierarchical orders (Darvish) that were somewhat akin to the cults and charismatic leaders of modern times. Each community had a prophet or an imam who ruled the small community by convincing his followers of his virtue while denying that he was seeking power. This was done through protecting the less powerful, following a modest life, and possessing supposedly supernatural abilities. There were numerous Sufi (darvish) orders, and their relationship with local political leaders was based somewhat on tolerance and possibly mutual respect. For the first time in four hundred years, people organized at the community level without significant control or even input from the central government.

Characteristics of Islamic Culture

To understand the attitudes, value systems, and social characteristic of Muslims during this era, we can consider some of the well-documented personalities: Muhammad ibn Musa al-Khwarizmi.

A Zoroastrian, Khwarizmi (c. 780 — c. 850) was born in Khorasan. His love of learning took him to the urban schools, where he encountered al-Mamun, the future caliph. To earn his title, Mamun had fought a bitter civil war against his half brother; Mamun's victory was only possible with the effective help of Iranian military support. The victory further alienated the traditional Arab tribesmen and solidified the concept of Iranian Islamic identity as an indigenous Iranian phenomenon.

After taking power, Mamun consolidated his rule. To compensate for the loss of Arab support, he gained the support of Iranian communities by encouraging the development of schools. When Mamun moved to Baghdad he attracted scholars and prominent religious personalities from all over the empire by engaging them in debates and discourse at the newly constructed Beit al Hakam, or House of Wisdom. This was probably the first governmental attempt at the mass conversion of Iranians to Islam.

The Islam preached at that time was a pragmatic religion heavily influenced by the Mu'tazilah school of thought. It represented liberation from the dogmatic, cleric-dominated, and irrational practices of the old religions of Iran. As such, it appealed to the more educated and rational members of the society.

Strong economic activity sustained numerous learning institutions throughout the empire. The schools helped to replace the simple tribal Arab religion with a sophisticated, tolerant, and cosmopolitan social contract that gave its members the freedom to engage in discourse about all aspects of life, existence, and the role of divinity. Exploration of arts and culture was encouraged. The pursuit of pleasures in life, which had been restricted to nobles in Sasanian times, became available to all.

The egalitarian social order opened all the previously forbidden pursuits of education and the accumulation of wealth to all its members. These openings in the social order made possible an amazing surge in human growth. A Muslim man of this era was empowered and in fact encouraged to use his intelligence and abilities to live his life the way he wanted, to engage in any social activities he desired, and to learn as much as he wanted. This personal empowerment of Muslim men distinguishes Islam from all other religions of the period.

In was in this intellectual and religious atmosphere that Khwarizmi moved to Baghdad, where he could pursue his studies with many more like-minded Iranians. Together, their contribution to knowledge and human growth was enormous. The establishment of the House of Wisdom systematically engaged numerous exceptional individuals from all social ranks of the empire by giving them the ability to pursue their dream while empowering them to live the life they wanted to live. These principles were the sources of the strength of Islamic society.

The debates with other religions' scholars effectively demonstrated the Islamic approach to social problems. A Muslim man of this era usually had the ability to rationally choose his profession and a life that he could envision for himself. In contrast, Zoroastrian and Christian men of this period were born into a social class and remained there, because God had ordained it. Given these realities, Islam must have been very attractive, especially to those in society who needed freedom to survive. It is through the empowerment of these people that social progress and development occurred.

The opportunity to learn through rational Aristotelian deduction became available and accepted in Muslim cities. It's possible that these new realities attracted those who were naturally inclined toward learning opportunities (perhaps the 2.5 percent of the population in Rogers' curve). It's also possible that these newcomers found their way to cities along the trade routes of the Islamic economic network. Hubs of higher learning attracted exceptional individuals who were not content with their social station in life, desired a different lifestyle, or had questions and were seeking answers. At learning centers, they had the freedom to engage in academic exploration of any type. This freedom proved powerfully attractive.

At the time of Khwarizmi's death in 850 CE, the House of Wisdom in Baghdad was a well-established center of higher learning. It attracted people from across Iran, including scholars such as Razi (865 to 925 CE) and Farabi (872 to 950 CE). By studying the life of these prominent scholars of the time and through their commentaries and treatises, we can learn about the social realities of the time. Farabi became well known among medieval Muslim intellectuals as "The Second Teacher;" that is, the successor to Aristotle, "The First Teacher." Farabi was a renowned scientist and philosopher of the Islamic Golden Age. He was also a cosmologist, logician, and musician. Farabi enjoyed good wine and lived a life full of pleasure, pursuing his instinct free from fear of prosecution by religious zealots. However, the lifestyles and more "liberal" social attitudes of Islamic scholars were not accepted by all.

By 950 CE, Islam had become the dominant religion of Iran. The caliphate was the center of Islamic activities, although politically the caliph's rule was merely symbolic. State power was diffused among local and national dynasties and strongmen.

From 946 CE, the Buyid kings, who happened to be followers of Shia Islam had ruled Baghdad, changing the caliph at will. Still, the state lacked the central organization of the Sassanid empires of the past. The Sassanid power structure had depended on the distribution of power across the social caste system. At the seat of state power was the Shahanshah, from whom all other powers received their authority and legitimacy.

Under the Buyid kings, Islamic government had a diffuse power structure. Political power resided in the local sultan, or shah, a term used for the first time since the fall of the Sasanians. In the distant corners of the empire, local strongmen held power over their communities. The caliph was the source of legitimacy for the established centers of learning throughout the empire, but increasingly local imams and charismatic cult leaders were competing with the caliph. Rather than a strong central government, these communities were linked by established economic connections and a network of human activities.

A Serious Challenge to Rational Thinking

In around 930 CE, about two hundred years after the establishment of the first school in Basra, a serious challenge appeared to Mu'tazilah, the dominant view of Islam. This new interpretation of Islam was launched by Abu al-Hasan al-Ash'ari.

In contrast to the rational approach of Mu'tazilah, the Asharite view of Islam held that:

1. Complete comprehension of the unique nature and attributes of God is beyond the capacity of human reasoning.
2. Although humans possess freedom of intention (not free will), they have no power to cause any action in the material world, as this is entirely the province of God.

This doctrine is now known in Western philosophy as occasionalism.

In addition, the Asharite view held that moral truths must be acquired by means of divine revelation. Human reason in and of itself could not establish any truth with absolute certainty, be it in respect to morality, the physical world, or metaphysical ideas. It was, however, permissible for a Muslim to believe and accept that a proposition is a moral truth based solely on the authority of a consensus of authorized scholars *(ulama)*. This is known in Islam as *taqlid,* or imitation.

The timing of Asharite articulation of these concepts coincides with a very important social reality: the acceptance of Islam by the majority of the Iranian public. A predominately Islamic society needed a different system of rule, one that provided more certain social control.

However, the decline of the Islamic Golden Age and the "rational observation of nature" was not immediate. The era would peak over a hundred years later in the middle of eleventh century. Academic progress and the development of Islamic learning institutions peaked with two giants of world renown, Ibn Sina and Abu Rayhan al-Biruni, both of whom had been inspired by Greek thought. Their contributions to medicine, astronomy, physics, geology, philosophy, theology, and numerous other fields are everlasting and incalculable.

The social transformation of the first four hundred years of the Islamic history of Iran (seventh century CE to the eleventh century CE) is an amazing study of the impact of social institutions on individual growth, achievement, and human development. Those exceptional Iranians who enjoyed the freedom and community support necessary to develop their unique abilities had a pivotal impact on human history and consciousness. This impact occurred not as the consequence of military might, but primarily as the result of societal support for individual creativity, persistence, and entrepreneurship.

For over four hundred years during this period, Iran's sociopolitical system supported learning centers that produced, promoted, and sustained a high level of scholarship based on rational discourse and human deduction free from state-approved interpretations of "truth." In fact, an amazing tolerance for contrarian views existed in Iran during this period. The influence of Iranian scholarship extended far beyond Iran's borders. Iranian scholars' contribution to humanity remained unsurpassed for many centuries afterward, until the Renaissance in Europe.

Still, in the Iranian empire, the "state" remained highly disorganized. By the eleventh century, there was a reverse relationship between the expansion of Islam and the control of the central government. Various cult orders and groups spread across the vast area of the Islamic network, nominally under the authority of the caliph. The Sufis, Malamati, Fotovvat, and Karamatih were the main groups and orders. There were also many other *madhhabs* (religious sects) from various forms of Shia (Ismaili, sixth imam, and others) as well as Khawarij and other Sunni schools. The office of caliph increasingly became a center of ceremonial ritual with no real power.

From its inception, the structure of the Islamic empire had experienced difficulties with the concentration of power. Umayyad rule, based on a system of tribal connections and patronage, dissolved after a few generations following some minor revolts. Abbasid power, based on wealth and purchased loyalty, soon degenerated into local systems of power. No central government had managed to achieve control.

In the eleventh century, the caliph's office was increasingly becoming irrelevant even in his remaining sphere of influence: religious matters. The majority of the population turned to different *madhhabs* as their source of religious authority.

With the caliphate weakened, Iran was a vast society that held tremendous wealth yet lacked a government capable of security or the ability to raise an army for its defense. This untenable power vacuum must have been alarming to Khwaja Nizam al-Mulk, an amazing Iranian statesman, who understood the need for a governmental nervous system that could react to aggression and threats. Indeed, this fragmented power structure could not even protect itself against the internal threat of a cult of assassins.

Nizam al-Mulk perceived that in order to build a strong central government, Iran needed a coherent, unified set of religious beliefs and unified learning centers under government control. His Nizamiyyah higher learning centers replaced the unorganized and decentralized approach to scholarship. The most famous and celebrated of all the Nizamiyyah schools was Nizamiyyah of Baghdad (established 1065), where Khwaja Nizam al-Mulk appointed the distinguished philosopher and theologian Abu hamid Muhammad ibn Muhammad al-Ghazali as a professor and leader of the school.

Ghazali has sometimes been referred to by historians as the single most influential Muslim after the prophet Muhammad. Ghazali was given the unique title of Hujjat al-Islam, meaning "The Proof of Islam," a title given to no other scholar or personality in Islamic history until that time. However, it is used as a lower ranking to Ayatollah in today's Iran, further displaying Ghazali's status within the religion. Ghazali contributed significantly to the development of a systematic view of Asharite theology and the integration and acceptance of it in mainstream Islam. He was a scholar of orthodox Islam, belonging to the Shafi'i school of Islamic jurisprudence and to the Asharite school of theology. Furthermore, he is known by some as being, literally "the man who saved Islam."

Ghazali's eleventh century book *The Incoherence of the Philosophers* represents a sharp retort to the more rational and scientific views of Mu'tazilah and Ikhwan al-Safa, as well as to the influence of Aristotle and Plato, whom Ghazali viewed as corrupters of the Islamic faith. Instead, Ghazali provided vigorous support for occasionalism, the concept that all causal events and interactions are the immediate and present will of God.

Ghazali's *Revival of Religious Sciences* adopts a similarly occasion-alistic view of the traditional Islamic sciences: *fiqh* (Islamic jurispru-dence), *kalam* (theology), and Sufism (philosophic/emotional view).

Ghazali also played a major role in integrating all forms of Islamic understanding that had emerged out of the social changes of the past five centuries, along with Iranian identity and experi-ence, into sharia. He combined the conceptualization of Sufism with sharia law. He was also the first to present a formal description of Sufism, an Iranian experience, as an integrated Islamic religious phenomenon. His works played a role in increasing the influence of Sunni Islam *fiqh*.

Ghazali is viewed as the key member of the influential Asharite school of early Muslim philosophy and the most important refuter of Mu'tazilites. However, he chose a slightly different position in comparison with the Asharites; his beliefs developed not only from the orthodox Asharite school, but also from his need to create an ideological background for the construction of the strong central state that he needed to protect the empire.

The breadth of Nizam al Mulk's work in this regard was amaz-ing: in addition to supporting Ghazali, he further commissioned Omar Khayyam and others to start a campaign of rehabilitating the Sasanians' political system, especially the Anoushiravan reforms. In fact, "Nizam al Mulk" was an honorific title meaning "good order of the kingdom" in Arabic. Nizam al Mulk's reforms were intended to create a strong central state that could withstand leadership changes. A critical element of these reforms was the idea of creating a strong civil-servant class that would be hereditary and would serve the ruler, whoever that might be. His effort to build a strong state remained unfinished, however, when an assassin, perhaps a member of a cult or a Darvish that Nizam al Mulk was planning to bring under control of the State, assassinated him.

Nizam al Mulk was correct in his assessment of the empire's security needs. Within five years of his assassination, the Crusaders, a ragtag army of European peasants with a small contingent of knights, successfully invaded and captured the western part of the Islamic empire.

At the time, Nizam al Mulk's goal of a strong centralized state was not possible. In fact, the push for a strong central government had the opposite effect: local leaders became even more independent from the office of the caliph even in religious matters. Instead of requesting interpretation from the office of the caliph, local leaders interpreted sharia, the newly formed laws themselves, effectively becoming the religious authority. The loss of a central religious authority further fragmented the empire, and local government structures became more independent of each other.

The reforms to the educational system, however, lived on. The rulers of the Islamic world started a campaign to cleanse the Nizamiyyah schools of freethinkers. The rational observation of nature and theology was abandoned and banned. Instead, the learning institutions became centers that advocated a particular view of Islam. They defined the role of a good Muslim according to the sharia laws. Contrarian views were not tolerated.

Sharia also empowered existing local rulers to become more tyrannical and to suppress any freethinking within their realms. The execution of Shahab al-din Suhrawardi sometime between 1191 and 1208 in Aleppo can be viewed as the high point of state intolerance. It represented serious changes in rules regarding previously held rights of free expression and personal interpretation of reality.

Suhrawardi, the master of oriental theosophy (shaikh-i-ishraq), may have expanded the horizons of the project to rehabilitate the Sasanian period. His efforts went beyond the perceived utilitarian political purposes into a new realm of consciousness. Iranians could well have identified with his analogies, which presented the three pillars of Iranian wisdom in a mystical realm. Suhrawardi actually undertook the renaissance of ancient Iranian wisdom, a project described as "reviving the philosophy of ancient Persia arising out of the Aristotelian philosophy as developed by Ibn Sina." Suhrawardi's illuminationist philosophy is critical of some of Ibn Sina's positions and radically departs from Ibn Sina in the creation of a symbolic language (mainly derived from ancient Iranian culture or Farhang-e Khosravani) to give expression to his wisdom *(hikma)*.

Suhrawardi was executed in 1191 0r 1208 CE following charges of cultivating Batini teachings and philosophy. Al-Malik al-Zahir, the son of the famous Saladin, ordered his execution without any attempt to get approval for such act from the office of the caliph. Suhrawardi could have been a transformative figure for this period. Given freedom, he could have created a synthesis that brought powerful Iranian cults and governmental authority together in one place. His execution was a clear indication of fundamental changes in Islamic society. From tolerance of alternative views, Iran was moving to a culture of intolerance and despotism driven by an expansionist Islamic rule insecure about any new interpretation of its core beliefs.

In short, Islamic sharia was a tool for the powerful to prevent social change and maintain their power. Initially, the appeal of Islam had been its pragmatic, logical, and rational observation of nature. Its security was its simplicity and its tolerance of different ways of life. This transformation to obsession, insecurity, and intolerance in time weakened Islam's appeal to seekers of knowledge and put the religion in the hands of political power brokers. In the twelfth century, Ibn Rushd published a lengthy rebuttal of Ghazali's *Incoherence* entitled *The Incoherence of the Incoherence*; however, the epistemological course of Islamic thought had already been set, and therefore the promotion of more rational thought was not possible.

About ten years after the execution of Suhrawardi, the worst fear and concerns of Khwaja Nizam al Mulk came in the form of Mongol attacks from northeast of the empire. Iran had organized a military force to repel the invaders, but the victorious Mongol army easily penetrated one urban area after another.

In order to secure their rapid advance and prevent uprisings, the Mongols, whose numbers were relatively few, resorted to massacring urban populations. To effectively maintain security, an advancing army needed about 30,000 troops to control each million of the conquered population. The best numerical estimate for Mongol forces attacking Iran was between 150,000 and 200,000. Therefore it would have been impossible for them to maintain their rapid advances and to provide for a secure line to their home base. Instead, they chose to massacre the populations they conquered. Within a few years, most of Iran's cities, which were also the major hubs of its economic network, had been annihilated. It is estimated that over five million Iranians, or about 40 to 50 percent of the population, lost their lives. Eleven major urban areas were destroyed, and all learning centers were wiped out.

Roughly a 100 years, later starting in 1383, these problems were exacerbated by another invasion from the east. Timur, a Turkic ruler from Central Asia, attacked and destroyed the urban areas that had escaped the wrath of Genghis Khan. By 1390, Timur had completed his invasion of Iran, leaving a ruined, depopulated, and impoverished country behind.

The lasting economic impact of the invasions by the Mongols and Timur reduced Iran to systematic poverty below the subsistence level for many centuries to come. More than 700 years later, this region has still not returned to the powerful cultural and economic position it once held.

Internal Change

The Safavid dynasty ruled Iran from 1501 to 1722 CE. Its founder, Shah Ismail I, was the Sufi leader of a popular cult. He later converted to Shia, and made this conversion mandatory for the largely Sunni population of Iran. All cities now in economic decline had to submit to Ismail's rule, and Sunni *ulama,* or religious scholars, were either killed or exiled. Ismail I brought in mainstream Ithna'ashariyyah Shia religious leaders from Iraq and Lebanon. He did so to create an ideological background for the creation of a new state using sharia, and fusing it with Shia fiqh, or jurisprudence. In practice, this was different from the sharia employed by the Ottoman empire, which had also adopted sharia and the office of caliph. Unlike the Abassid caliph, the Ottoman caliph combined political and religious authority in a single person.

Ismail I granted the Shia ulama land and money in return for loyalty. These scholars used the sharia laws that developed with Shafii fiqh in previous centuries, which drew on Sunni Islam. However, the underlying fiqh was altered to Shia fiqh. An interesting point is the fact that the Safavids themselves belonged to a Sufi order but made a rational calculation for political purposes to adopt Shia.

Later, during the Safavid and especially the Qajar dynasty

(1785-1925), the power of the Shia ulama increased. They were able to exercise a role independent of or compatible with the government. Despite the Safavids' Sufi origins, most Sufi cults were brought under government control or were prohibited.

Under Shah Abbas (1571-1629), Iran did experience some economic growth, but in general it never enjoyed the kind of sustainable economic success that could lift it from the perpetual poverty that was endemic across Iran from the Mongol invasion until the middle of the twentieth century. Poverty was the most intractable of the social problems that beset the nation.

The imposition of Shia based sharia law forced all other forms of religious affiliation underground and offered a constant rebuke to the authority of the rulers. Forced sharia veiled the entire social fabric of the society and helped create a culture that mistrusted any authority. The poverty and alienation proved almost as difficult to define as they were impossible to cure. This was the age before social science and social medicine, when there was still no standard definition of poverty and no clear sense of who was and was not poor. Nor were there serious attempts before the twentieth century to assess the extent and pervasiveness of poverty. The assumption that poverty was a problem for governments to address lay far in the future. Instead, an almost obsessive concern with security and social control dominated the ruling class.

The European Impact

Two decisive events in the fifteenth century sealed the fate of Iran for centuries to come: the fall of Constantinople to the Ottoman Turks in 1453 CE and the successful journey of Christopher Columbus to the Americas in 1492.

The capture of Constantinople by the Ottoman Sultan Mehmed II in 1453 CE, fulfilled an 800-year dream of Muslims, whose many attempts to control the city had produced only failure. This victory consolidated the position of the new caliph, combining the office of caliph and sultan under Islamic law. Soon afterward, all institutions of higher learning under Mehmed's domain were closed, and all Islamic schools became centers of study for Islamic fiqh.

For Europeans, the fall of Constantinople made travel to the Orient by traditional routes difficult or even impossible. In the past, European merchants had sailed to Constantinople and traveled overland to India and China to get silk and other trade goods. The loss of Constantinople to the Ottomans closed this important gateway to the East and prompted European merchants to seek other ways to get the commodities they needed.

The fall of Constantinople weakened the Eastern Orthodox Church and indirectly strengthened the power and the prestige of the Pope in Rome. This created an urgency to push out the last Muslim state from western Europe, leading to the Granada War and the fall of Muslim Granada to Spain.

Granada fell in January 1492. Its fall created an opportunity for Christopher Columbus, whose attempts to finance a voyage in search of a new route to the Orient had been turned down by European leaders. Flush with Granada treasure, Isabella and Ferdinand of Spain financed Columbus' expedition, which reached the Americas on October 12, 1492.

The impact of Columbus's voyage on the course of human development and especially on Iran was great. The infusion of the vast economic resources of the New World into the European market made the poverty and disparate living conditions of the majority of Iranians even more pronounced.

The situation was exacerbated by yet another invasion of Iran in 1722, by tribes of Pashtun Afghans, which led to the collapse of the Safavid dynasty. The looting, killing, and destruction in Isfahan and many other urban areas, as well as the civil wars that followed, once again reduced the economic conditions of Iran to below subsistence level.

European's ocean voyages, their gradual domination of the New World, and their oppressive treatment of conquered peoples caused a shift in European attitudes toward other peoples of the world. The demands of rapid growth, economic wealth, and the need to build new tools and weapons forced a new form of awareness on them. To meet these demands, Europe was forced to develop.

Primarily, knowledge transferred from the Muslim world served as the vital raw material for Europe's scientific revolution. Muslims not only passed on Greek classical works, but also introduced scientific theories they had developed on their own, without which the European Renaissance could not have occurred.

In Europe, the main social transformation occurred in the nineteenth century, the hundred years of relative peace from defeat of Napoleon at Waterloo in 1815 to the start of the World War I in 1914. It brought about a social transformation unparalleled in human history.

The Age of Imperialism began in about 1900. It represented a major shift in human consciousness, and had a worldwide impact, as European powers raced to take control of new colonies in Africa, Asia, the Middle East, and the Americas. Understanding the impact of this era on the Muslim world, on Muslim consciousness in general, and on the Iranian experience in particular is the key to understanding the current problems in Iran.

During the Age of Imperialism, Iran experienced rapid economic decline in comparison to Europe. It also experienced a feeling of powerlessness, as its resources were exploited by outsiders. Iranians became conscious of their poverty, and actual declines in living conditions created a situation of dependency. Iranians lost their self confidence, and a good portion of the control of Iran's economy was consigned to Europeans. Iran became an exporter of raw material and all manufactured goods were imported, along with some social customs and behaviors.

Human progress has never been linear or confined to one race or geographical area; all humanity has contributed to it. This unacknowledged truth has played an important political role late in the twentieth century and into the twenty-first. The emergence of Orientalism as a cultural reality further reduced the possibility of Iranians' seeing human cultural achievements as their own and has allowed them to create a distorted view of themselves. The existing political climate of mistrust and hostility toward the West may possibly be correlated to a sense of humiliation and frustration on the part of Iranians. It has prevented the integration with and sense of ownership of human progress. To build trust, Iranians need to share and to be participants in future humanity and receive acknowledgment for their contribution to human achievement.

There are major schisms in the history of the Iranian identity, its social significance, and the manifestation of it in everyday political behavior. The historical "facts," have been generated not by a cultural self-examination, but by imposition from outside. We have to be suspicious of this information, since, like all nineteenth century European ideas, it is tainted with the chauvinistic ideas of the time. Such information primarily satisfied the needs of its creators. In contrast, Iranian social values and feelings are implicitly national. These values drive the nation by implementing policies that are sometimes hard for outsiders to understand and difficult to analyze rationally.

In Iran, for over 800 years, the persistence of abject poverty, consecutive massacres of the population, famine, despotic leaders, and sharia prevented the development of the indigenous analytical capabilities necessary to acquire an internal historical perspective. The twentieth century brought Iran a social revolution of constitutional democracy, followed by a civil war. Soon afterward, it was dragged into an unwanted World War I followed by famine, cholera, and Spanish influenza all in a span of less than twenty years. During this time, Iran lost close to 40 percent of its population. Disasters capable of destroying a nation have been a normal way of life in Iran for over 800 years. What has held Iran together is an emotional bond among its people and a sense of common destiny.

The New Iran

"The New Iran" was the slogan of Reza Shah, who came to power in 1921. Many works of European historians became available in Iran for the first time. The European scholars of this era presented Cyrus the Great as an Aryan general similar to Julius Caesar or Alexander the Great who built the Iranian empire by personal ambition, the might of his army, and military domination. The noble Aryan Sasanian kings were defeated by Semitic Arabs who imposed Islam on the vanquished people of Iran.

This Western picture of Iranian history suffers from a confusing perspective. It paints a picture of the noble Aryan "Persian" Cyrus who brings order to the Semitic people. This gets more convoluted and confused when fifty years later the noble Aryans become the herds of Asiatic despots who are invading the democratic, art-loving Greeks.

These distorted views come from the needs of Western civilization and its Orientalist perspective. In the New Iran, there was no Iranian perspective on history; in fact, there was no studying of history. The architects of the New Iran wanted to train engineers and doctors, not scholars. Most Iranians were content to see themselves as the Europeans did. But the contradictory historical views explained by a Western scholar relegated Iran to a state of collective schizophrenia.

In truth, Cyrus brought together the mighty civilizations of the ancient world. His campaign was for the most part peaceful, and he changed the world by bestowing simple values of coexistence. He did not consider himself a noble Aryan whom others must worship. He did not impose his language or his religion on others. He did not create *pax iranica* nor force others to use Persian customs as Alexander did. Cyrus's deeds created an Iranian identity, just as Moses created the Jewish identity during the Exodus. In fact, it is very likely that the story of Moses's Exodus was inspired by Cyrus's behavior. The Old Testament was created by the order of Darius some fifty years after Cyrus to give identity to the Jews. As far as we know, Moses is not a historical fact. There is no record of the migration of Jews from Egypt, but Cyrus is a historical fact. It is highly probable that the authors of the Old Testament were influenced by the story of Cyrus creating Iran.

Despite the attempt at imposing a Western civilizationist view on Iranian history, Iranians do not suffer from cultural schizophrenia. Islam was not imposed on Iran by force. The Arab armies who invaded Iran so long ago removed the Sasanian dynasty by force, but they did not impose Islam. The cognitive Iranian values helped promote the growth of simple Islamic seeds in Iran. Iranians used the economic prosperity and social freedom provided by Islamic cities to prosper and grow their own personal lives based on their own identity in a relatively free environment. This created an Islamic Golden Age, which was brought to an end by the imposition of sharia law, employed in an attempt to create political control.

CHAPTER TWO

A Brief History of the Modern State

The modern state is hugely important in our everyday lives. It takes nearly half our income in taxes It registers our births, marriages and deaths. It educates our children and pays our pensions. It has a unique power to compel, in some cases exercising the ultimate sanction of preserving life or ordering death. Yet most of us would struggle to say exactly what the state is.

— Christopher Pierson, The Modern State, 1996

The Rise of Europe and the End of the Islamic Golden Age

After the fall of the Roman Empire, the political structure of Europe between the fifth and fifteenth centuries was chaotic and vulnerable to continued invasions.[1] Given this political instability, cultural achievements in the first five centuries of the Middle Ages were limited. The outbreak of the Black Death in 1346, followed by other deadly diseases, fearsome famines, and wars provided the backdrop for the people of western Europe at this time. The Europeans of this period were constantly aware that life is precarious. Consequently, they set very little value upon human life, their own or that of others.

Society in general was very poor, food was scarce, and shelter was limited. The population competed for scarce resources and took huge risks for modest achievements. They knew that success was only temporary in these miserable social conditions; life was a risky endeavor. Discovering and conquering new territory was part of this risk — a desperate gamble for success.

The fall of the Muslim city of Granada (Gharnatah), on January 2 of 1492, to the forces of Catholic Monarchs Isabella I of Castile and Ferdinand II of Aragon, ended nearly eight centuries of Muslim rule of Spain and closed one of the most glorious chapters in Islamic history. The looted treasures of this conquest financed the voyage of Christopher Columbus and ushered in the age of discoveries. This violent end sealed the fate of tolerant, urban, and sophisticated Islamic societies. These events marked the end of medieval Europe and the beginning of the modern state. The age of mercantilism had begun and continued until the Europeans seized control of the world's seas, creating a global market and spreading their culture throughout the world.

An influx of gold and silver caused perpetual inflation in Europe. The basis of wealth in medieval Europe had been land, and the property owners lived well. Land rent was adequate, and tenants also provided the owners with labor and a share of their crops. The flow of precious metals flooding into Europe caused prices for commodities to soar. The landlords and property owners who were on a fixed income were impoverished, but the renters witnessed a drop in real value of their debts. Spain and Portugal, the countries acquiring most of the gold and silver, did not have sufficient manufacturing capacities, but they needed goods and supplies for their new dominion. The Netherlands, England, and France developed the manufacturing facilities to provide these goods and in later years became centers of industrial and financial productions.

The introduction of new crops from the Americas caused major changes in European agriculture as well. The medieval European had subsisted mainly on wheat and other grains. An acre of land that produced at best ten bushels of wheat could yield twenty to thirty bushels of maize. What the farmers did not use, they fed to livestock, thereby increasing the availability of meat. Potatoes, however, made the real difference. A single acre of land could produce 25,000 pounds of potatoes, enough for a large family with enough left over to feed a couple of pigs. Added to this were tomatoes, squash, pumpkins, beans, and other vegetables that arrived to vary the European diet.

The new colonies in America exploited other resources of the New World. Timber and wooden shingles, hemp rope, tar and turpentine, furs, dyes such as indigo and red Brazil wood, dried fish, flaxseed oil, hides, and many other raw materials supplied the growing industrial economy, enabling Europeans to build powerful military and transport ships. Very soon they dominated the world with their goods, used for trade with India and China. The discoverers and explorers were replacing land-owning nobility, and the manufacturers and merchants soon became the ruling class of Europe. In contrast, the decline of Iran and other Islamic countries continued. The defeat of the Ottoman army outside the gates of Vienna is regarded as the beginning of the decline of the most powerful Islamic country.

Emergence of the Modern State

Definitions of the modern state have evolved significantly over time, and the history of modern states reflects that trend. The sociologist Max Weber defined a modern state as a political community with an administrative and legal order, with binding authority over citizens and actions in its sovereign territory and the right to legitimately use physical force in its jurisdiction. [2] According to Christopher Pierson, the features of such a state include monopoly, territoriality, sovereignty, constitutionality, impersonal power, public bureaucracy, authority and legitimacy, citizenship, and taxation.[3]

The modern state has its roots in the vacuum created by the religious struggles of the sixteenth and seventeenth centuries.[4] With its conceptual roots in the treaty of Westphalia (1648) and the subsequent recognition of the concept of sovereignty, the actual emergence of the modern nation-states can be traced to eighteenth century Europe and in particular the removal of the absolute monarchies in France.

Eighteenth Century France

After Louis XIV dispensed with the role of the prime minister, he and his successors appointed ministers with discretionary power in highly differentiated functions. The "king's ministers depended upon the loyalties of particular families, clans, or cronies" and "the primacy of clique and family conflicted with political modernization and economic expansion" during the latter part of the eighteen century.[5] As a result, France's privileged classes — including the political elite — disintegrated into a multitude of factions. The rivalry and mistrust this cronyism engendered encouraged allegiance to particular ministries rather than to the regime as a whole, which in turn prevented the open exchange necessary for economic expansion. This allegiance was rooted in the feudal system, in which vassals pledged loyalty to a lord in return for use of land, and guilds tightly controlled trade on a local level. But by the eighteenth century, with the rise of opportunities for national and international trade, France had begun to move away from feudal economies. Over the course of the eighteenth century, France continued a transition that had been under way for at least two centuries, and moved toward a mercantile system.

Mercantilism is a term burdened with a sometimes contradictory array of definitions. In eighteenth century France, mercantilism meant the erosion of the "fiercely protectionist trading policies of towns and principalities by breaking down the barriers separating these two types of noncompetitive commerce . . . thus clearing the way for a national market.[6] As merchants identified and gained access to national and international markets, they began to press for unification of the state. The goal was to increase power in foreign affairs and encourage the accumulation of wealth. "Economically, the instrument of unification was capital, i.e., private resources available in forms of money hoards and thus particularly suitable for the development of commerce."[7] Yet while trade had been in one sense liberated from the municipalities and local craft guilds, it was not liberated from regulation. Protectionism played a role here, just as it had in the guild-driven feudal marketplace.

Simply put, the new mercantile system could not be separated from French culture and history. Economic relationships remained "submerged in general social relations," and even as the markets became more developed "as under the mercantile system, they thrived under the control of a centralized administration which fostered [absolute control] both in the households of the peasantry and in respect to national life."[8] These new markets certainly changed some forms of social and political structures and interaction, yet France was not yet ready to accommodate an independent economy.

Markets, as Heilbroner points out, whether they be exchanges between primitive tribes where objects are casually dropped on the ground or the exciting traveling fairs of the Middle Ages, are not the same as the market system. A market system is more than a means of exchanging goods; "it is a mechanism for sustaining and maintaining an entire society."[9]

During the eighteenth century, French mercantilism meant working to increase the overall wealth of society by aiding the expanding merchant class. The tools used to accomplish this were regulation and protectionism, but using these tools effectively required the formation of a stronger central government. Advances in science and technology, the growth of commerce, and recognition of the need for a more effective and centralized mode of regulation in both internal affairs and foreign policy converged to bring about tremendous change. Industrialization, laissez-faire economics, trade policy, and the construction of new civil and political orders were soon to be the major concerns informing both ideology and practice. Charles de Secondat, Baron de Montesquieu, significantly influenced the change.

The Spirit of the Laws and the Separation of Powers

Montesquieu wrote his epic treatise, *The Spirit of the Laws,* in 1748, as France struggled to meet changing internal and external realities.[10] A significant feature of his recommendations for sociopolitical reform was the now familiar concept of the separation of powers into the legislative, executive, and judiciary branches of government. His theories — and this concept in particular — would play a significant role in the formation of the United States government.

Montesquieu did not share the concern of political theorists such as Locke, who emphasized natural human rights, or Rousseau, who advocated law based on the "general will" of the people. And unlike the American patriots who would come later, the Baron was not a populist. He adamantly disapproved of direct democracy or the participation of the general citizenry in public debate, decision, or administrative action. It was clear, he believed, that the people ought to have no share in the government but for the choosing of representatives and that "as most citizens have sufficient ability to choose, though unqualified to be chosen, so the people, though capable of calling others to account for their administration, are incapable of conducting the administration themselves."[11] Neither was he a revolutionary, advocating the overthrow of the existing state. And although he opposed absolutism, the granting of total governmental power to one person or body, he was not anti-monarchial. He acknowledged the "sacred power" of the monarch but warned that monarchs can be corrupted and transformed into despots.[12] This can occur if the

monarch deprives cities or individuals of their rightful privileges.

Montesquieu began his discussion of the separation of powers by asserting that in order to achieve political liberty, "it is requisite the government be so constituted as one man need not be afraid of another."[13] In determining how to achieve this goal, he first described the three kinds of power existing in every government: the legislative, the executive, and the judicial.[14] It was imperative, he believed, that these three powers be housed in different persons or bodies. He considered the separation of legislative and executive powers especially important, because if these powers "were to reside in the same person or assembly, tyrannical legislation can be both enacted and executed with no opposition."[15] If the conditions of separation were not met, liberty as he defined it could not be achieved. Using the British Constitution as his model, he proposed the following governmental structure: First, the legislative power should be vested in two bodies: one representing the nobility, to protect its existence and privileges from "popular envy," and one representing common people. The latter branch should be elected not by "the general body of the nation," but by towns or districts where inhabitants "are much better acquainted with its wants and interests . . . and are better judges of the capacity of their neighbors."[16] The two legislative bodies thus served to protect and represent two classes and two different interests in society and assure that neither could disregard the other. Montesquieu also proposed that while the legislative and executive branches should remain distinct in their composition and powers, the executive must have veto power over legislative enactments. And while the legislature should not have a corresponding right to stay or prevent executive action, it should be able to examine "in what manner its laws have been executed."[17]

Although he believed in the divine right of kings and the authority of a hereditary nobility, Montesquieu addressed a number of issues that are still significant today: 1. recognition of the need for centralization in the conduct of foreign policy and war and in the regulation of commerce for economic growth; 2. the question of regional or sub-national interests in the national legislature; 3. the concept of a rule of law that should be recognized as upholding the interests of the monarchy and the nobility; 4. the separation of powers with a system of checks and balances; and 5. the role the people should play in a system of representative republicanism. Montesquieu, like Adam Smith, was writing in the eighteenth century, when the mercantile system was beginning to give way to ideas of entrepreneurship, expanded markets, and the need for a more centralized control of commerce to accumulate national wealth.

Montesquieu's ideas would play a major role in the writing of the United States Constitution and the development of the U.S. government. But it is important to remember that his ideas were not written with twenty-first century economies in mind. In 1748, economic institutions such as large multinational corporations that could rival nation-states in their wealth and power were not even on the horizon. However, one exception might be the British East India Company, which had incredible power and played a huge role in the oppression of the American colonies, and which led to the drive for independence. The company also exercised a great deal of control over British policy regarding India and China. The British East India Company was dissolved in 1874 as a result of the East India Stock Dividend Redemption Act passed one year earlier, as the Government of India Act had by then rendered it vestigial, powerless, and obsolete. Its functions had been fully absorbed into the official government machinery of British India and its private presidency armies had been nationalized by the British Crown.

The Founding of the United States

The ratification of the Constitution of the United States of America in 1789 marked the birth of a new nation, a new structure of government, and a new foundation for political discourse. Together, these created a new paradigm for the modern state. The United States employed a republican form of government that was yet untried. Its society remained relatively isolated from the British and Continental nations that had colonized it. Its economy was beginning to enter an age of industrialization and capitalism, influenced by Adam Smith's revolutionary work on economic theory, *The Wealth of Nations,* which had been published in 1776.

Before looking at the major facets of the debate that accompanied the founding of the United States, it is worth asking why the American state in particular assumes a place of such importance in a discussion of how the modern state developed. Although the colonists had shared national backgrounds, the conditions they faced in their newly appropriated territory were far different from those of the countries they left behind on the other side of the Atlantic Ocean. After well over a century on this new soil, they had developed their own set of social mores, traditions, principles, forms of commerce, industrial and agrarian practices, and political institutions. Separated by distance and an increasing sense that their interests and needs were neither understood nor protected by the governments that controlled them, part of the population developed a sense of alienation and resentment. Colonists forcefully expressed this sentiment in the revolutionary slogan "no taxation without representation."

While the colonies had a history of shared experience, it was neither uniform nor institutionalized in the same way as, for example, the history of England or France. The authors of the Constitution were not given a completely blank piece of paper on which to write, but they had more opportunity to break from convention and exercise creativity in the design of their new government. They could — and did — draw on a wide variety of old-world philosophers (including not only Montesquieu, but Locke, Rousseau, and others) as well as on their own considerable experience and intellect.

Finally, the colonization of America exemplified the worldwide economic changes taking place. The feudal system of industry, in which industrial production was monopolized by closed guilds, had become incapable of meeting the growing needs of expanding markets. "The manufacturing system took its place . . . and division of labor between different corporate guilds vanished in the face of division of labor in each single workshop."[18] Eventually, even this was inadequate, and manufacturing was taken over "by the giant, modern industry . . . [which] has established the world market, for which the discovery of America paved the way.[19]

We now turn to a brief overview of the principles, institutions, and relationships that the Constitution — and the new paradigm of the modern state — embodied therein. Many of the issues raised by Montesquieu were revisited in the debate over the United States Constitution. The Framers debated 1. the powers that should be vested in a central government and those that should remain with each individual state (each of which was much smaller in population than is the case today); 2. the separation of the executive, legislative, and judicial branches, the powers to be given to each, and the checks and balances each branch should have against the others; 3. the proper composition of the legislative branch; 4. the representation of individual states' interests at the national level; and 5. the ability of the general population to participate in the discussion and resolution of public issues.

In 1781 the newly independent colonies had established a "league of friendship," defined by the Articles of Confederation. But the Congress created by that document had little power. Its explicit purpose was the conduct of the war, and each of the thirteen new states retained their sovereignty and independence in all policy matters not expressly delegated to the Congress. This soon proved to be unsatisfactory, as the states printed worthless money, imposed tariffs on one another, and entered into separate treaties with foreign nations. Debtors unable to repay loans had their land and other property seized, and citizen unrest and revolt increased. Fearing mobs and anarchy, the colonies agreed to a convention that would define a more effective form of governance and security.

The delegates to the Constitutional Convention met in Philadelphia in 1787 to define the principles and structures of the new state. Its government was to be balanced, not by providing representation of different classes or "estates," but by "allowing the different components of a federal system — the people on the one hand, and the states on the other — to be represented in the central government."[20] Clearly there was a need for increased centralization, but how much and in whose hands? In approaching this question, Forsyth contends that the majority of the delegates agreed on three basic principles: 1. the people, not a "divine right," were to be the source of authority in the new republic; 2. a republican form of government should be based on the principle of election to office, not hereditary right; and 3. the basic concept of a separation of powers — legislative, executive, and judicial — should be adopted.[21]

Within this basic framework of agreement there were many differences of opinion regarding the manner in which the agreed-upon principles should be implemented. One area of disagreement concerned the elective principle and the role of the people in the selection of federal officials. As the fear of a tyrannical monarchy faded, and in the face of widespread discontent and rebellion, a possible "tyranny of the majority" became a consideration. And should a majority of the "common people" — those with less education, less property, less social status, less power — prevail, the status of the privileged minority would be endangered.

Because legislative power was considered the most potent, the plan for election of members of Congress proved especially problematic. Following Montesquieu, the delegates decided that there should be two houses — not only to check one another from ill-considered legislation, but also to provide representation from two different bases. The upper house, or Senate, would equally represent each state; regardless of population each state would have two senators, and those senators would be chosen according to a manner determined by each state legislature. Members of the House of Representatives, the lower chamber, would be apportioned on the basis of population and directly elected by the people of each state. This legislative scheme solved two problems: It provided a buffer between the people and the selection of senators, and it provided a compromise between states with smaller populations (mostly northern and industrial) and those with larger populations (mostly southern and agrarian). The smaller states benefited from equal representation in the Senate and the larger from the proportional representation of the House of Representatives.[23]

The executive should be carefully limited both in the extent and the duration of its power. But precisely because the legislative branch must predominate in a representative system, its powers are more subject to abuse. The possibility of such abuse was addressed in part by the separation of legislative power into two chambers with different modes of election and with the requirement that both chambers approve proposed legislation before its enactment. The weaker executive, on the other hand, needed fortification so as not to be overshadowed and rendered powerless. This justified the inclusion of the presidential veto, or the president's right to kill legislation deemed unworthy. The veto could only be overridden only by a two-thirds majority in both the Senate and the House.

The presidential selection process sparked debate about the degree to which the people were capable of direct participation in elections. Delegates devised the Electoral College, a body unique in both its composition and procedure.[24] It represented yet another dilution of democratic representation.[25] The Supreme Court, in which the federal judiciary power was vested, was even further removed from the electoral process. Because of the expertise and impartiality required of the justices who were to be the arbiters of the Constitution (and thus of the constitutionality of federal legislation), they were to be appointed by the president with the "Advice and Consent" of the Senate.[26]

Basic Principles of the United States Constitution

The Constitution was adopted in 1788, slightly over a year after the delegates to the Constitutional Convention began their deliberations. As this cursory overview has shown, the primacy of the representative principle and a republican form of government — but not a direct democracy — were upheld. Power was not concentrated in one person or body but separated among the legislative, executive, and judicial branches of the central government, with each branch exercising checks on the others. Furthermore, both the national and the state governments retained sovereignty in their separate spheres. "Power" at the time was considered an attribute of government, and it was dispersed on the basis of this assumption. Economic entities that might need regulation and control as major political entities were not yet part of the scene.

One crucial provision remained missing from the Constitution as ratified: a written statement of individual rights protected from infringement by the national government. One of the first acts of the newly installed government was to pass and send to the states the first ten amendments to the Constitution. The ratification process was completed by December 1791, and the Bill of Rights was implemented. Added to the representative and republican principles, the limitations on the concentration of powers, and the retention of sovereignty at both the national and state levels, the guarantees of individual rights protected from encroachment by the national government succeeded in forming the foundation of a truly "new modern state."[27]

Several points should be noted. First, the Bill of Rights drew its theoretical heritage not from Montesquieu but from Locke and Rousseau, both of whom also upheld the right of the people to establish a new government if the principles of natural law and individual sovereignty were violated.[28] This concept found expression in the personal "freedoms" associated with religious expression, speech and press, the rights of persons accused of crimes, "due process of law," and other liberties spelled out in the Bill of Rights. The Tenth Amendment specified that all powers not specifically given to Congress are reserved for the individual states. This attempt to prevent the federal government from usurping the states' sovereignty of the new nation also made the Constitution unique.

However, the Commerce Clause, located in Article III of the Constitution, has been used over time to shift more and more power to the federal government via judicial review. Ironically, this power —to regulate commerce with foreign governments, among the states, and with the Native American governments — was intended in part to provide the kind of centralized government regulation and control deemed necessary in the movement from mercantilism to the modern state. Today, it seems fairly clear that the Framers did not anticipate the tremendous power inherent in judicial review of legislation. But the Commerce Clause has been used time and time again in judicial decisions that expanded the scope of federal authority and correspondingly limited the powers of state governments.

The United States Constitution, and the Bill of Rights in particular, gave citizens of the new modern state guaranteed liberties and rights that protected them from abuse of power by the federal government. However, in conjunction with the Commerce Clause, the Fourteenth Amendment (1868), and other Constitutional provisions, elements of the Bill of Rights also helped provide for an expansion of federal government power that could not have been foreseen by the original Framers. With far-reaching consequences for the modern state, provisions of the Bill of Rights originally intended to protect individual rights and liberties have been extended to the "artificial persons" known as corporations.

The Bill of Rights represented an uneasy compromise between proponents of direct democracy and those who feared "the tyranny of the majority." It also highlighted a concept of human rights as "natural" or "inviolable," derived from the essence of humanity itself rather than from a specific government or set of laws — a concept that many of the Founders reluctantly endorsed. And as industrialization and a concomitant concentration of wealth and power grew in the fledgling United States, a new stage in the discussion of rights began. From the 1820s through the Civil War years, Americans on the margins of power — wage earners, women, slaves, and artisans — who were affected by the new system of wage labor and capital organization began to think seriously about "socially constructed forms of power" and to "turn to the language of politics to express their sense of injustice."[29] These groups joined members of the anti-slavery movement by making claims cast not in terms of

Constitutional or legal rights, but of "natural rights" against "everyday tyrannies of capital, bosses, slave masters, and husbands.[30]

The Thirteenth Amendment, passed after the Civil War ended, effectively abolished slavery in the United States. But even with the added "protection" of rights intended by the Fourteenth and Fifteenth Amendments, eleven states were able to impose segregation and the effective denial of legal rights (including the right to vote), and failed to recognize the "natural" rights accorded to all humans.[31] Similarly, the rights demanded by wage earners remained generally unrecognized, and women would wait until the passage of the Nineteenth Amendment in 1920 to gain the right to vote.

Beginning in the 1870s and extending into the 1930s, the courts became players in what Rodgers has termed "a wholesale construction of new property and entrepreneurial rights."[32] The right of free contract was used against workers — overturning laws aimed at protecting labor. Maximum working hours, minimum wages, and other protections were struck down as interfering with the very mechanism of a free market system. This was the period of "high industrial capitalism, massive immigration, business consolidation, and bitter and continuous labor conflict."[33] The courts relied repeatedly on the theory of rights established in the Constitution to defend the interests of capital and of corporate entities, which they began recognizing as a special type of "artificial entity" with the attributes of personhood.

"Rights consciousness" continued through the Great Depression, bringing about innovative federal legislation to help the poor and the unemployed, and protections for workers' health, safety, and economic benefits. From the mid-1950s through the mid-1970s, civil rights legislation and Supreme Court rulings expanded the rights of blacks in the United States, ending the fiction of "separate

but equal" in educational and other public facilities. Various
state laws aimed at preventing blacks from voting — literacy
tests, poll taxes, and "grandfather" clauses — were declared
unconstitutional and federal marshals were sent to some southern states to ensure that black citizens could register and vote. By
creatively combining the Commerce Clause with the Fourteenth
Amendment, the Supreme Court also found unconstitutional the
segregation and denial of service on the basis of race by privately
owned facilities such as hotels, restaurants, and other facilities
open to the public.[34]

Other groups began to make claims for equal rights, as
evidenced by the Women's Movement that arose in the 1960s
and '70s. Increased control over reproductive functions, more
equity in the workplace, and the ability to buy property without a husband's consent are only a few examples of the rights
gained by American women. The rights of disabled or "differently
abled" people, in the form of equal accessibility to government
and private services and employment, began to be recognized.
And the Supreme Court constructed a "right to privacy" from a
"penumbra" of other rights specifically mentioned in the original
ten amendments of the Bill of Rights.[35]

In this respect, then, the promises of the Bill of Rights and other
sections of the Constitution guaranteeing rights and liberties seemed
at last to be applied to formerly disadvantaged groups in U.S. society. It was not an easy accomplishment, and the results cannot be
discredited; this cursory overview only hints at the struggles endured
and the gains achieved. It was individuals, acting alone and in asso-
ciation, who sparked the amazing social changes of the mid to late
twentieth century. As the Supreme Court has become more conser-
vative in its composition (beginning in the 1980s), its decisions have

in some cases contracted rather than expanded individual rights and liberties, but society as a whole has continued to benefit from the gains in civil rights attained during this era.[36]

In summary, the founders of the American republic did not predict, and could not have predicted, the new power structure that was in part the product of industrialization, the concentration of capital, changing conceptions of commerce, and the new market system. As the United States matured, as its governmental powers were modified and reinterpreted, as societal conditions changed along with the growth of new economic institutions, the original "balance" so important to its founders was lost. Today, the socioeconomic condition of the country reveals how these rights led to the economic developments of the past two hundred years. The individual protections afforded by the new society fostered opportunities that led to amazing innovations and technological advances. But during the nineteenth and twentieth centuries, corporations became a dominant form of economic organization. As laws were changed and the Constitution was reinterpreted to meet the demands of a changing society, corporations began to assume the legal rights and immunities once intended for individual citizens.

CHAPTER THREE

The Modern State at a Crossroad

Too remote to manage the problems of our daily lives, the nation-state nevertheless remains too constrained to confront the global problems that affect us.

— Jean-Marie Guéhenno

Why have the political and economic institutions created to meet problems faced by inhabitants of the eighteenth, nineteenth, and early twentieth centuries not adapted — or been adapted — to meet the needs of contemporary societies? Although there have been modifications and analytic reinterpretations, the fundamental assumptions and consequences of the modern state have remained for the most part not only accepted, but accepted without serious challenge. And in fact, because it has not evolved along with societal conditions, the modern state is creating a dysfunctional environment for its citizens and has begun a downward spiral that must be addressed to assure the survival of healthy individuals, productive and fulfilling social relationships, and viable political and economic systems.

The governmental structures exemplified by the new American state were instituted over two centuries ago. It was impossible to foresee at that time the conditions that characterize the twenty-first century. Yet this does not mean that these structures are obsolete or should be abandoned. Their effect on human living conditions, individual creativity, and fulfillment of human potential has been both extensive and positive. But they must be adapted to retain their vitality and to continue the improvement of life throughout the world.

To explain why the modern state has not changed, it is necessary first to:

1. define the assumptions and characteristics of the modern state
2. explore how the modern state can encourage creativity and enhance the quality of human life in both "developed" and "developing" nations, ensuring its own survival as well as the health of the planet;
3. understand why government regulation continues to grow at the expense of economic prosperity and individual initiative; and
4. investigate the reasons why the modern state has been so resistant to change.

With the disintegration of the Soviet Union and the formation of the European Union, the modern state has been arguably in decline. The notions of sovereignty and independence are more and more giving way to regionalization and interdependence.[1] There are many reasons for the decline of the modern nation-state, but in this chapter we will look at some of those factors that curtail the ability of a modern state to advance the welfare of its citizens. First, we will explore how corporate "citizenship" has undermined the democratic process in modern states such as the United States. We will then look at the changing nature of conflict, security, and sovereignty through various lenses. Finally, we will look at the ineffectiveness of modern states to address local and global issues of interest to their citizens in the twenty-first century.

The Modern State and Corporate Rights

As with the rights of individual citizens, corporate rights — those assigned to the "artificial persons" of corporations — developed in tandem with changing social and economic realities. And as with claims for individual rights, corporate rights moved through different phases or stages of identification and implementation.

The American Revolution marked the end of the mercantile system and ushered in the market system. Because of its tradition of individualism and opposition to government interference, the United States provided fertile soil for Adam Smith's preindustrial capitalism and laissez-faire approach to the economy. As the nineteenth century approached, a growing industrialism made possible by the division of labor and a faith in unrestrained competition put Smith's theory to the test: as corporations became a more significant factor in economic activity, the relatively new government was asked to define both corporate rights and the degree of regulation to which corporations would be subjected. At the time of the nation's founding, corporations were created by state charters, and had only those rights granted to them by state authority. Corporate rights could be modified and corporate charters terminated at the will of the state.[2]

This tight control over corporations was soon relaxed. As early as 1819, the United States Supreme Court described the corporation as an "artificial being" with the right to enter into contracts.[3] Furthermore, as an "artificial being," property of the corporation could not be disposed of at the state's whim once it had been created. This limit on the state's authority provided the basis for an expansion in corporate autonomy and power, especially as corporations began to grow as a popular way of doing business.[4]

In 1886, the Supreme Court verbally addressed the issue of whether corporations had the rights of people. The Court reporter recorded the statement of Chief Justice Morrison R. Waite as follows: "The Court does not wish to hear argument on the question whether the provision in the Fourteenth Amendment to the Constitution which forbids a state to deny to any person within its jurisdiction the equal protection of the laws applies to these corporations. We are all of opinion that it does."[5]

The Court did not formally rule on the issue of corporate personhood. But from this point on, Jess Krannich argues, the Court has assumed — using a variety of metaphorical descriptions — that a corporation is a person. It has done this despite its failure to establish a test to determine what a Constitutional person is or whether a corporation meets such a test.

With this assumption of personhood in place, the legal rights of corporations have been steadily expanded, and the ability of government (either state or federal) to regulate corporate activity has been steadily diminished. This has led to a widespread belief that:

> The rise of the modern corporation has brought a concentration of economic power which can compete on equal terms with the modern state — economic power versus political power, each strong in its own field. The state seeks in some aspects to regulate the corporation, while the corporation, steadily becoming more powerful, makes every effort to avoid such regulation. Where its own interests are concerned, it even attempts to dominate the state. The future may see the economic organism, now typified

by the corporation, not only on an equal plane with the state, but possibly even superseding it as the dominant form of social organization.[6]

A recent decision of the United States Supreme Court illustrates how far the revolution in corporate rights has come. In January 2010, overturning previous decisions, the Court ruled that the government cannot ban political spending by corporations (including media corporations) in elections for office.[7] "If the First Amendment has any force," Justice Anthony M. Kennedy wrote for the majority "… it prohibits Congress from fining or jailing citizens, or associations of citizens, for simply engaging in free speech." Joined by the three other members of the court's liberal wing, Justice Paul Stevens said the majority had committed a grave error in treating corporate speech the same as that of human beings.

While the opinion did not affect bans on direct contributions to candidates, dissenters questioned whether there is a meaningful difference between donation to candidates and independent expenditures on behalf of candidates (including candidates in judicial elections, who may play a large role in settling disputes between individual citizens and corporations). "The difference between selling a vote and selling access is a matter of degree, not kind," Justice Stevens wrote. "And selling access is not qualitatively different from giving special preference to those who spent money on one's behalf."

This decision must be considered in the context of dramatic increases in corporate spending for the congressional elections of November 2010. In 2010, soon after the Supreme Court's decision, more than $300 million was budgeted for the campaign by a group of fifteen conservative tax-exempt organizations.[8] While liberal groups also are heavy spenders, "the momentum and the new money appear — at least at this moment — to be coming from business and its allies."[9]

Corporations are growing in size and in wealth at the same time that they are being accorded expanded rights. Based on a comparison of corporate sales and country GDPs, corporations represent 51 of the 100 largest economies in the world; countries represent only 49. Further, the top 200 corporations' sales are growing at a faster rate than overall economic activity. Between 1983 and 1999, corporations' combined sales grew from the equivalent of 25 percent to 27.5 percent of world GDP. While the sales of the top 200 corporations are the equivalent of 27.5 percent of world economic activity, they employ only 0.78 percent of the world's workforce. U.S. corporations dominate the Top 200, with 82 slots (41 percent of the total).[10]

In light of these findings, it is important to ask how the increased size, wealth, and political impacts of corporations affect the representative republic originally envisioned for the United States. Will corporations wield such influence in informing the public on issues and candidates that they effectively can determine election outcomes? Will the predictions that corporations may equal and even supersede the power of government be realized? Will citizens of the United States lose even more confidence in the legitimacy and effectiveness of their political institutions? These questions cannot be adequately answered here, but they are important considerations in any attempt to envision an alternative vision of the modern state.

Sovereignty, Human Rights, and Regionalization

Sovereignty experienced its most radical growth in the post-colonial era of the twentieth century. The overwhelming majority of the countries in the world are considered sovereign nations. Between 1945 and 1989 more than one hundred sovereign nations were added to the list of nations, and another twenty were born between 1989 and 2001.[11] At the same time the concept of sovereignty has changed significantly since the initial days of the modern state. Adam Tokar identifies two types of sovereignty, external and internal.

> *A state is [externally] sovereign if it is acting independently on the international scene and recognized by others states (not necessarily all other states). There is another, just as traditional meaning to the term, and that is "internal" sovereignty. Internal sovereignty means the existence of a single, stable and supreme state power structure inside the boundaries of a state, unchallenged by other actors. The extent and limits of internal sovereignty are far less clear than those of external sovereignty. The German Democratic Republic of the 1980's directing virtually the entire economy, massively endorsing an almost religion-like state ideology, controlling the private life of its citizens by a huge secret police force was just as sovereign a state as any liberal democracy of the West. What can be said almost with certainty is that probably no state has ever exercised complete rule over its territory; but, to be sovereign, a state must be able to secure a public order on its territory, respected by the overwhelming majority of the population.[12]*

In the twenty-first century, the distinction between domestic and foreign affairs is starting to blur. One example is the threat of nuclear meltdown subsequent to the 2011 Japanese earthquake and tsunami. Such disasters affect not only the country in which they occur; the effects are worldwide. In addition, the use of force as a means to enforce sovereignty and resolve conflicts among nations is giving way to self-enforced compliance with agreed-upon rules of collective interaction and behavior. The compliance with European Union rules by member states is a good example of how the sovereignty of countries is compromised to further the interest of those nations in a larger union.

The ability of information technology to transcend political boundaries has made political borders and territorial sovereignty even less relevant. Additionally, common vulnerabilities represent security issues for many nations, prompting collaboration and interdependency as ways to ensure their existence. Traditional use-of-force strategies play a smaller role.[13] All of these factors are undermining the main advantages of the modern state, which has relied heavily on the concepts of territoriality and sovereignty as its reason for being.

The issue of human rights (both individual and collective) is one of the most challenging issues for contemporary state sovereignty. Claims based on human rights often challenge the ultimate authority of the state in both legal and political matters. The increase in traditional and social media coverage of human rights violations has made it harder for the international community to look away when atrocities occur. The recent case of the indiscriminate attack of the government of Libya on its own citizens (throughout March 2011), and the protective military response of the United Nations Security Council underlines these emergent changes.

"In cases when a crime is committed by a state:

1. all other States are under a double duty (a) 'not to recognize as lawful the situation created by the crime' and (b) 'to cooperate with other States in the application of measures designed to eliminate the consequences of the crime';
2. all States may claim to have an interest to lodge claims

before any international available mechanism; a crime creates a possibility of an *actio popularis* which normally does not exist under international law;

3. contrary to the usual fundamental principle prevailing in international law, the 'veil' constituted by the State can be pierced and the international penal responsibility of the officials, including the Head of the State, is entailed (this is not so for all other international wrongful acts committed by a State: in these cases officials enjoy 'jurisdictional immunities' (the ongoing Pinochet case is a striking example of what is at stake here); and

4. 'counter measures' (this is the new terminology for reprisals) can be taken by all other States against the wrongdoer, and the conditions for these counter-measures are considerably softened."[14]

This would suggest that as we progress into the future, fundamental human rights will be increasingly held to be universal, and systematic violations of such rights will not be protected by national sovereignty claims.

The Changing Nature of War and Conflict

Since the collapse of the Soviet Union and the emergence of large regional economic and political blocs such as the European Union, the balance of power principle that gave rise to the recognition of sovereignty in international relations has become increasingly irrelevant. The September 11, 2001, attacks on U.S. soil and the subsequent wars in Iraq and Afghanistan, along with the recent uprisings in the

Arab countries for greater democratic rights have changed the nature of international relations.

The "war on terror" is quite different from the conventional wars for which nation-states were structured. These wars typically ended with the defeat of an opponent, a cessation of hostilities, and some kind of formal document to denote the end of the conflict. In the war on terror, however, there is no specific battlefield and no clear end to the conflict. The enemy is not a formal military force. This kind of war has no boundaries and is directed against multiple enemies from (often undefined) locations around the world.

This new paradigm for war poses a major challenge, since adversaries are mixed in with friendly or at least non-hostile populations. Different segments of a population within and across sovereign borders, not two or more individual nations, are pitted against one another. Self-organized, fragmented adversaries are often more agile in conducting asymmetric warfare. They may be capable of leveraging information technology to organize in ways that are difficult for traditional intelligence-gathering institutions to penetrate. None of the institutions of the modern state are well equipped to deal with this paradigm of warfare. In fact we would argue that the only way to combat it is within communities themselves. Without the cooperation and support of communities, it will be close to impossible to address this challenge effectively.

Manifestations of Inequality

In the United States, the new modern or neoliberal state peaked and then began an uneven decline in the last two decades of the twentieth century. At its height, the United States was considered a model for democracy characterized by: 1. an open, participatory government that balanced safety and security with individual freedom; 2. institutional safeguards against tyranny; 3. unprecedented civil rights for its citizens; and 4. equal opportunity, if not equality in fact, in both its political and economic spheres. Continued economic growth and an increase in the standard of living were widely believed to be both natural and inevitable. As capital accumulated, investment and production flourished, unemployment fell, consumers consumed, and the economy grew. Successive waves of innovation changed not only available tools and techniques but also human consciousness. Modifications have occurred in our understanding of the way the world works, our place in it, and our relationships with other people. The development of power sources, means for transporting goods and people, and methods of communication resulted in a globalization which the modern state has not yet been able to handle effectively.

Thomas Friedman[15] argues that successful government and policy now depend on a recognition that the world has become increasingly leveled and flat. He views some of these "flatteners," made possible in large part by rapid advances in computer technology and high-speed communication, as new forms of collaboration:

1. "Outsourcing," or moving parts of an organizational operation to wherever it can be accomplished most effectively, efficiently, or cheaply;
2. "Offshoring," or moving an entire production facility from one part of the world to another;
3. "Open sourcing," or development of products or systems with free or nearly free labor in order to duplicate and undercut dominant competitors. (Friedman uses the example of Firefox, a web browser that became

a freeware alternative to Internet Explorer. It was developed through collaboration between two people
— one at Stanford, one in New Zealand — who had
never met.)

But as the world flattens, and new forms of communication
and collaboration for creativity emerge, economic conditions in the
United States have worsened for many of its citizens. David Kotz[16]
lists three important developments that have contributed to this
situation: 1. growing inequality; 2. a financial sector increasingly
absorbed in speculative and risky activities; and 3. a series of large
asset bubbles. The "DotCom" bubble that burst late in the twentieth
century encouraged investment in real property. The resulting real
estate bubble then was followed by a collapse in the value of mort-
gage-related securities, creating economic and political havoc and
bringing untold homeowners to the brink of financial ruin. This, he
argues, led to a "systemic crisis:"[17]

> However effectively a particular institutional form . . . may for
> a time promote high profits and economic expansion, eventually the
> contradictions of that form . . . undermine its continuing operation,
> leading to a systemic crisis.[18]

While corporate wealth has increased, the financial situation of
the average person continues to decline. The business cycle from
2000 to 2007 is the only one in the post World War II years in
which median real household income was lower at the end than at
the beginning, due in large part to: 1. rates in corporate profit growth
that outstripped rates in compensation growth and 2. increased
rates of worker output per hour that exceeded rates of growth in

compensation per hour.[19] During this same period, the perceived economic expansion "was driven by consumer spending that rose more rapidly than GDP, rising from 68.7 percent of GDP in 2006 to 70.3 percent in 2007.[20] Consumers financed this spending by refinancing their homes, often with variable-rate mortgages and other risky loans. Forty percent of American families' home equity disappeared between December 2006 and December 2008, while unemployment hovered around 10 percent.[21] As a result, household debt (mortgage debt plus credit card debt) as a percentage of disposable personal income rose to an astonishing 128.8 percent by 2007.

As corporate size, wealth, and rights have grown disproportionately large, so too have the gaps between those at the top and those at the bottom of the income distribution, with fewer and fewer Americans controlling more and more of personal income. Even taking into account "income taxes and government benefits and private health insurance and pensions roughly 40 percent of all household income gains over the last generation, from 1979 to 2007, went to the richest one percent of Americans."[22] Remarkable advances in technology alone, despite increases in productivity, have not been able to stem the tide of income inequality or corporate power.

The technological innovations of the past three decades have caused a flattening of the three important components of the capitalist economic system — markets, information, and capital — making them more accessible to all human societies. It is becoming apparent that individual creativity and innovation are the most important forces for future social change. However, the existing political model can not further this social change and development. The power of corporations and institutionalized trade unions create inequalities in the social setting and obstacles to the free development of individual initiatives.

In other words, when there is a failure in normal problem-solving
(consistent with the dominant paradigm), crisis occurs and new theo-
ries emerge . . . The significance of crises is the indication they provide
that an occasion for retooling has arrived . . . All crises begin with the
blurring of a paradigm and the consequent loosening of the rules . . .
And all crises close with the emergence of a new candidate for a para-
digm and with the subsequent battle over its acceptance.[23]

Declining Public Confidence

While a linear correlation between income and electoral behavior
has never been demonstrated, voting studies over the past half century have shown a strong correlation between voters' perceptions of
their economic situation and prospects and the way they cast their
ballots.[24] The major influence of wealth — whether it be that of
corporations or of the small percentage of the population that receives
the highest incomes — is the unequal access it provides. In an age of
multimillion-dollar elections, party selection of candidates, campaign
spending, media advertising, and electoral outcomes are dependent on
raising money. When relatively few people provide a majority of this
money, their influence over policy decisions is magnified. Congressional votes or administrative decisions may not be bought directly,
but the largest players in the game of political finance at least gain an
advantage in terms of their access to key decision makers.

While individual voters may not understand the source of the dispar-
ity between expressions of popular opinion and policy decisions, they
are aware of its existence. This in turn can create a general feeling
of discontent and frustration. Not surprisingly, this discontent and

frustration has affected citizen participation in and citizen attitudes toward government and politics in the United States. The election of 2008 showed a massive swing in votes from the Republicans to the Democrats. And while midterm elections often show a backlash against the presidential party, those in 2010 displayed an unusually large rebound in favor of Republicans. Furthermore, the Tea Party movement that emerged in the 2010 elections appears to have been formed and supported by people who had little in common other than unhappiness with their personal economic status. This demonstrates not a profound change in ideology but massive confusion and dissatisfaction with things as they are. Voters, despite their declarations, are voting not so much for or against specific policy issues as they are to improve the conditions of their lives.[25] News of the social discontents and economic problems of democracies like the United States are daily conversation for the rest of the world and are often used by other governments to justify their own undemocratic political systems.

The complicated web of political and economic factors outlined above can not be neatly separated. What is suggested, at the least, is that many American citizens are disillusioned, distrustful, and angry about conditions they believe government could solve if only it had the will and willingness to listen to their voices. What seems without question is that in some fundamental way there is a growing and potentially dangerous disconnect between the ideal of a representative democracy as understood by its citizens and its actual operation.[26] Most Americans have an ingrained expectation of "equality," although that concept is understood in different terms depending on one's "place" in society. When expectations of equality and its correlate of hope for a better life — however these terms are understood — are violated, people look for someone or something to blame.

It is easy to believe that something has gone awry in the United

States, whether or not one agrees with Arianna Huffington's assessment that America is in danger of becoming a "Third World" country with only two classes — the rich and the poor — and a government totally ineffective in the face of a greedy corporate elite.[27] This is both a political and an economic crisis: one coin with two sides.

The Brink of Crisis?

The modern state is characterized by national control of foreign relations and of commerce, a separation of powers, federalism, and a constitutional guarantee of individual rights and liberties. For over two hundred years, this state has been remarkably successful in providing a secure environment and in fostering the individual initiative and creativity that provide for self-actualization and contribute to the public good. Now, however, due in part to a concentration of rights, resources, and power in the hands of large corporations, and to a lesser extend trade unions, the modern state is on the brink of crisis, "a growing sense, often restricted to a segment of the political community, [that] existing institutions have ceased adequately to meet the problems posed by an environment that they have in part created."[28]

Our argument is that the reality of the twenty-first century — marked by dramatic and rapid technological change, increased inequality (limited access to the political process for individuals and greater access for wealthy corporations), and decreased confidence in existing political institutions and processes — calls for dramatic political change. Therefore any attempts to use this model for Iran and MENA countries must address these concerns. Traditional tools of monetary and fiscal policy, for example, will not be sufficient to redress the existing imbalance in economic conditions of these countries. Similarly, it will be difficult to address inequities in political influence and power especially in societies that do not have developed social or legal institutions. We believe that meaningful change can be effected only through conscious, volitional human action in the development and pursuit of a shared vision or a model that can address the existing social problems facing democracies that are not more advanced. The current crisis may precipitate social change, but individuals will be its agents of change in an uncertain future. In times of crisis, increasing numbers of individuals become increasingly estranged from political life and behave more and more eccentrically within it. Then, as the crisis deepens, many of these individuals commit themselves to some concrete proposal for the reconstruction of society in a new institutional framework.[29]

When it becomes impossible to resolve existing problems from within the existing traditional institutional framework, it is necessary to step outside that framework, to envision an alternate set of structures and processes, and to present that vision for consideration of others within the political community of these nations. Before explicating our vision, we will consider current signs of imminent crisis and the possible application of modern state government and examine the role of the community in encouraging and stimulating individual and public vitality.

Maury Klein contends that technology, defined as "tools and techniques for accomplishing some task":

1. has played an important role in developing vast resources to achieve information and material gain;
2. is value neutral, neither inherently good nor evil, to be used by the people or in the hands of government agents;
3. may often result in "unintended consequences" that

were not foreseen or were dismissed by the original inventors and innovators.[30]

The vastness of the American frontier and its abundant natural resources provided opportunities — both social and environmental — that encouraged individual creativity and innovation. In Iran and other MENA countries it is the abundance of information and visions of other possibilities that will drive the concept of personal liberty. The accumulation of capital, in modern states made possible in part through the institutionalization of the corporation as an organizational form, encouraged investment and entrepreneurial activity. Although inequality certainly was present in the first two centuries of the United States' development, the belief in and possibility of equality and individual advancement existed on a previously unknown scale. Similar aspirations, although a different situation, is evident in emerging nations. The diversity of immigrants to modern states created a "brave new world,"[31] that broke the bonds of traditional and insular thinking and opened the way for an exchange of ideas. Similar future possibilities cannot be expected for emerging countries such as Iran where this type of diversity does not exist. However, the increasing flow of global information has changed the perspective of many Iranians in the past two decades. At the same time, improved transportation and communication has allowed the Diffusion of Innovation to spread much more quickly than had formerly been the case.

Creativity, Innovation, and Community

Creativity, invention, and innovation were part of the soul of the new modern state. Many of the first inventors were "tinkerers," without scientific background or knowledge.

Some of the first steam engines and boats were invented by men who literally had never seen a steam engine, didn't know what one was or have any theoretical knowledge of it. They just fiddled and faddled and came up with something.

On the other hand, you had not really scientists as such but well-heeled people who were interested in nature and theoretical questions, who had the time and money to pursue in intellectual terms the nature of heat and electricity.32

Economist Joseph Schumpeter[33] stressed the importance of innovation for society, claiming that labor and capital alone were unable to sustain economic growth and increase productivity. Innovation was the critical factor in avoiding a stagnant economy or in pulling an economy out of what could otherwise become a permanent depression or recession. He identified five different kinds of possible innovation:

1. a new good;
2. a new method of production;
3. a new market (one that had not existed or been previously entered)
4. use of a new source of raw materials or partially manufactured goods; and
5. a new organization of industry (e.g., a monopoly).

Innovation was the province of entrepreneurs, who would provide the financing and expertise necessary for implementing the innovation and stimulating productivity. Its continuation was assured by a process termed "creative destruction." New technologies sometimes modified or furthered the application of existing ones but sometimes threw out the old and established a new. There would thus be an enduring and ongoing cycle of technological innovation and change, guaranteeing continued economic growth.

Schumpeter distinguished between "competitive capitalism" and the "trustified capitalism" that he saw emerging in the pre-Depression years. Under trustified capitalism, innovation became the province not of individuals but of research and development labs in large corporations, often with funding from the federal government. The problem with this "trustification," as he diagnosed it, was that innovation would be artificially directed to enhance profits for a particular firm or to further interests (e.g., defense) defined by the government, stifling creativity by limiting the free expression of individual imagination and talent.

In order to exercise fully their remarkable capacity for creativity and innovation, humans first must satisfy two categories of basic needs: the need for security and the need for significance. Security derives from knowing that adequate food, housing, health care, public safety, and other basic conditions for human life are available and accessible. Significance refers to a belief that one's activity is both purposive and valued and can be achieved by engaging individual talents and capabilities in a way that is useful or meaningful to other members of a community. Achievement of these basic needs — security and significance — requires cooperative action and mutual support.

Although creativity often has been viewed in terms of the character or personality traits of highly innovative or brilliant people, this conception ignores the communal, cooperative, and mutually supportive aspects of the creative process.

The power of the unaided individual mind is highly over-rated. Although society often thinks of creative individuals as working in isolation, intelligence and creativity result in large part from interaction and collaboration with other individuals. Much human creativity is social, arising from activities that take place in a context in which interaction with other people and the artifacts that embody collective knowledge are essential contributors.[34]

A fully developed view of creativity requires recognition of the human need for individuals to be engaged with each other in various kinds of social networks that provide the essential ingredients of security and trust. To accomplish this, the environment of corporate dominance and exploitation must be replaced by one in which there is equal access to power and wealth and in which the pursuit of individual talents and goals is encouraged. Only then can the full force of individual creativity, initiative, endurance, and imagination be captured for community achievement and progress.

Many fundamental human services such as health care, education, housing, employment, emergency services, infrastructure, and crime control are provided at the local level or in collaboration with other locales. Local dependence on national funds for providing and delivering these services often has created inequality and inefficiencies within and across locales.

At least two major problems are created by a national-level response to community issues. In culturally and ethnically diverse countries the national government is unable to customize many of its services for different locales and different populations. Empowering local communities can create a fundamental shift toward greater efficiency, effectiveness, and transparency in community-level services.

Local governance is not without problems of its own, however.

Much advocacy of decentralization sees virtue in moving as much governance action as possible towards such smaller units of population, in the belief that this will be the best way to mobilize citizens to participate in the management of their collective affairs. In a globalizing world, it is inevitable that Schumacher's (1973) "small is beautiful" axiom will have much appeal, and community in this sense serves it well. But there are negatives as well as positives.[35]

Communities may be "the source of the ethical values that make a wholesome civic life possible," but, "if they become too strong, [they] breed identity politics, and with it the potential for social division, or even disintegration."[36] While the "almost mythical image of the benign, united, knowledgeable community" has great appeal, communities sometimes are beset by "ignorance, disunity, ethnocentricity, authoritarianism, corruption, and ineptitude."[37] In moving toward decentralization and effective community governance, it is important to take these potentially negative possibilities into account as well.

A Vision for Change

For Iran and other MENA countries to adapt the existing model of the modern state without considering the recent past experiences of human suffering caused by this model would be totally irresponsible. The objective should be to learn from the achievements and mistakes of this model as it has been developed and to try to address these deficiencies in envisioning a new political model that can theoretically address these problems.

The technological innovations of the past three decades have allowed three important components of the capitalist economic system — market, information, and capital — to become more accessible in all human societies. It is becoming evident also that the most important forces for future social change and development are individual creativity and innovation. However, the existing political model, that of the modern state, cannot further this social change and development. The power of large corporations and trade unions creates an inequality in the social setting and obstacles to the free development of individual initiatives.

As a first step, we argue that the successful postmodern state must find a way to level the playing field in society and redress current inequities in the power structure. To accomplish this, we would retain some of the precepts of the modern state while suggesting new structures and processes designed to halt the trend toward corporate dominance and provide all individuals equal access to public resources. We believe that the values underlying the federal system, the separation of powers, and the protection of individual rights and liberties are important and should be preserved. The structures that embody those values, however, should be modified to prevent as much as possible the undue concentration of community resources in the hands of an elite. With this objective in mind, we propose a community-centric government coupled with a four-branch central government.

The modern nation state as conceived in the eighteenth and nineteenth centuries and strengthened in the twentieth century is becoming less capable of meeting the needs of diverse constituencies. At the same time, the modern state and the democratic processes that govern it have begun to be challenged by corporate interests and the weakening of traditional sovereignty. Now we must consider whether it is possible to reform the modern state or if a paradigm shift toward an alternative governance structure is necessary.

CHAPTER FOUR

Community, Human Creativity, and Democracy: Manifesto for a Community–Centric Government

"In the Virtuous Community, citizens come together and cooperate with each other in order to become virtuous and attain happiness. With objective knowledge and the ability to distinguish between the virtues and the vices, man can ultimately reach perfection. The community's concerted efforts develop the virtuous states of character from which emerge the noble activities useful for achieving happiness."

—Farabi (tenth-century philosopher) Excerpts from Charles E. Butterworth[1]

Introduction

Across the Middle East and North Africa (MENA), people are coming together to demand the fulfillment of basic human needs. They are insisting on individual freedom, decreased inequality, and meaningful participation in the decisions that affect the conditions of their lives. Resistance to oppressive governmental structures is occurring in almost all MENA countries in one way or another. However, even the successful toppling or collapse of one regime and its figureheads will not necessarily lead to structural changes that satisfy these demands. Western liberal democracies, long a model for democratic transitions in the rest of the world, are facing their own set of existential challenges and might not offer an ideal pathway for MENA nations to follow. This manifesto espouses the idea of bottom-up community-centric participatory democracies that foster individual and communal creativity, growth, and prosperity.

In June 2009, hundreds of thousands of Iranians took to the streets to protest what they deemed to be significant election fraud committed by the ruling establishment of the Islamic Republic. The goal of the fraud, the protesters contended, was preventing the prospects of a democratic transition in the country. Despite the apparent failure of the so-called Green Movement to bring about a democratic transition for the Iranian people, their demands for greater freedoms resonated across the Arab world. The protests were a predecessor to the wave of social and political upheavals that is permanently changing the political landscape of the region. Dubbed the Arab Spring, this change is probably the most expansive geopolitical transformation of the past seventy-five years, following the division of Europe after World War II, and represents both an unprecedented opportunity and a significant threat. With the rise of political Islam as an alternative to secular authoritarian regimes in most of the MENA countries, the prospect of transition to democratic governments that are respectful of human rights is problematic.

In moving toward a democratic future, the conventional strategy has been for those in MENA to look at Western liberal democracies as a model. However, liberal democracies in their current form face their own set of existential challenges. The global financial crisis that started in 2008 demonstrated the inability of modern liberal democracies in Europe and North America to protect the prosperity and welfare of their respective populations. The alliance of national governments with powerful, global, private interests, and a lack of rigorous oversight resulted in global financial institutions taking unprecedented risks. These risks, in turn, led to the second-largest worldwide economic collapse in history, exceeded only by the Great Depression of the 1920s and 1930s.

Government responses to the collapse, including the bailout of financial institutions with public funds and austerity measures that severely cut public goods and services for the most vulnerable portion of the population while protecting the wealthy, have led to large-scale protests. The unexpected scope of the Occupy Wall Street movement in the United States and the street protests against austerity measures and unemployment in Greece, Italy, the United Kingdom, Israel, Spain, and Brazil demonstrate the depth of the dissatisfaction and frustration that citizens of liberal democracies feel toward their governance structures, creating a crisis of legitimacy. Whom do the governments of these democracies represent and protect?

To explore this question, we can look at the example of the United States. There, selective access to and exploitation of public resources has created wealth for corporations and for those who control them at the expense of the general public. At the same time, this unbalanced relationship has reduced and limited the availability of opportunities for growth and for the innovative use of these same resources by other motivated individuals.

The culture and strength of America's shrinking middle class has been eroding. Corporate size, wealth, and power have increased rapidly, often at the expense of smaller, more entrepreneurial companies. Today, corporations control over 90 percent of the wealth (assets) in the U.S., and have an undue influence on its national elections. The federal government wields tremendous power yet fails to meet the needs of its citizens, while elected officials have become increasingly focused on raising funds for the next election and meeting the needs of the corporations that provide those funds. It has descended into a morass of partisan bickering and stalemate. Local governments have more potential for providing the flexibility and responsiveness their citizens need, but even these abilities are being constrained by the federal power structure and a lack of resources.

The problems of liberal democracies have an impact far beyond their borders. At this point, human ability to sustain the Earth is seriously threatened. Growing populations, declining natural resources, increasing corporate power, and the inability of central governments to respond to the needs of the people are symptoms of this threat. The abundance of natural resources we have enjoyed during the past two centuries has been drastically reduced and is disappearing. Preservation of what remains will require continuous management. Correct and responsible management of these resources will become an essential requirement for the future availability and enjoyment of the world's wealth and treasures. The interconnectedness of the world also provides opportunity. As resources decline and options narrow, technology and people-power make possible a responsive, community-centric government that can solve critical problems and create prosperity for a much broader section of the population than ever before.

With highly concentrated urban populations, traditions of communitarian social structure, and weak governments in dire need of replacement or repair, the nations of MENA provide the ideal place for the birth of this new governmental structure. In order to capitalize on this, the people of MENA must learn from the experiences of Western democracies, work harder to understand the cultural context of their own societies, and explore new ways to make democracy work. It may be time for the region that gave birth to the oldest human civilizations to set an example rather than to follow one. Sects and tribes can be positive social structures if they are used as trust networks. For the most part these societies do not have a developed civic society with an accepted rule of law. However, these old societies do have strong communities that are organized based on traditional values. The effective use of existing trust networks such as these is perhaps the only possible way to build lasting democracies. Engaging these collectives in the administration of community governments can be a positive force for change.

This manifesto espouses the idea of creating a new form of community-centric participatory democracy to foster individual and communal creativity, growth, and prosperity in Iran and other MENA nations. Like society during Iran's Golden Age, the new system will employ the power of local economies in which people are given freedom to exercise creativity and entrepreneurial skills as they see fit. Community-centric democracy will help create a healthy collaboration of creative individuals that is greater than the sum of its parts. In addition, a shift from a centralized resource system to a community-centric power structure can lead to direct participatory democracy and increased accountability among local governments. While the focus of the proposed model is on Iran and the MENA region, the general principles underlying the discussion are applicable to a wide range of societies.

Participatory Democracy Versus Liberal Democracy

Liberal democracy emphasizes citizen participation in government through free and fair elections of representatives in a competitive political process. While representation of citizen interests is essential in a democratic system of governance, elections alone are not sufficient to define democracy. To define democracy as elected representation alone reduces the rights and responsibilities of individual citizens to voting for public officials in election cycles.

The current legitimacy crisis in Western liberal democracies stems in part from structural issues that reduce the power of individual citizens and undermine the democratic process. Here we will briefly mention a few of these issues and their implications for democracy.

- *Disempowerment of the citizen.* The democratic process in liberal democracies has reduced the citizen to a passive voter. The entire political process revolves around marketing, manipulation, big-budget advertising campaigns, and the formation of spurious "grassroots" groups — all designed to entice voters to cast their votes for one candidate/party or another. Once the elections are over, many citizens cede control to their representatives, who are not accountable to their constituents until the next election and even then are protected by large campaign war chests. This situation mocks the democratic process. True democracy entails political accountability as well as direct participation by citizens in determining the conditions of their lives. While representation is a key aspect of democracy, representation alone is insufficient.
- *Co-option of government by special interests.* The concentration of political and economic power in the hands of large organizations, especially corporations that have been given unprecedented legal rights, has impeded individual development and created a huge inequality in the distribution of resources.

- *Large-scale bureaucracy and procedural inefficiency.* The centralized nature of resource allocation in liberal democracies requires a massive bureaucratic structure to collect the data and information necessary for the provision of services at the local level. The transaction cost for such an effort is prohibitive and often ineffective, because federally developed solutions may not mesh with local conditions in all areas. The context present at the community level is difficult to translate to the national level, and many opportunities are lost by top-down interventions that undermine the capacity for local problem solving.

In contrast to liberal democracy, participatory democracy focuses on the broad, active participation of people in the political structure and decision-making processes. It allows all members of the community to make meaningful contributions to decision-making that affects their lives and the allocation of their collective resources. In practice, participatory democracy is only possible at the local level, as the scale of issues and the complexity of problems at the national level makes the participation of people in national issues challenging. There is no one better suited to identify what needs to be done to improve the quality of life in a community than community members themselves.

Iran and MENA: An Ideal Opportunity

The cultural and geographic diversity of cities in the MENA region provides a unique opportunity for social and economic competition and collaboration that encourages sustainable development. Located in a semi arid/arid region, the population of the MENA region is concentrated primarily in the geographical areas surrounding cities. This concentration of social, political, and economic life has expanded over the past two centuries, and urbanization is continuing at an increasingly fast pace. It is time for the urban centers of MENA to combine participatory democracy with their traditional economic strengths to foster creativity, entrepreneurship, and growth.

How might this work? In more industrialized areas, local governments could focus their resources on attracting more industries or enhancing services. Local governments in different economies might focus on tourism or services; still others might look to attract educational and research centers. Turning historical rivalries into drivers of sustainable development will spur mutual prosperity for the citizens of these cities and result in greater prosperity for the country as a whole. Collaboration between cities on particular issues can also produce mutually beneficial results. Cities can pool resources, share information, and create competitive blocs to compete with other cities around the nation, the region, and the world. The community-centric governance model is compatible with the MENA region's rich urban history, natural geography, and current sociopolitical realities. Rather than the poor adaptation of an existing Western form of governance, it builds on the communitarian culture of the region.

Principles of the Community-Centric Governance Structure

The proposed system of community-centric democracy relies on strong local governments working together with a lean, effective, and strong central government to meet the needs of people. The division of labor in such a system will ensure that issues that are truly local can be addressed effectively at the local level, while issues that are national and international in nature can be handled by the central government with much less bureaucracy.

The term *local* in this context primarily refers to the geographic boundary of a city, its suburbs, and surrounding towns and villages. In a community-centric democracy, local governments will be directly responsible for the everyday well-being of their citizens, while the national government will deal with issues of national defense and other large-scale policy matters. This will allow citizens to be involved more directly with issues of immediate interest to them. It will also lead voters to judge competing political parties more by their performance on specific, practical matters rather than by their promotion of abstract ideologies.

The critical difference between a community-centric governance model and a centralized administrative structure is in the allocation mechanism for public resources and the respective government revenue models. Unlike a centralized structure, in which all resources are distributed top-down by the national government, resource allocation in community-centric democracies will happen primarily at the local level. The local government will have direct budgetary and policy authority, and a strong central government will support the economic growth of local governments while it deals with issues on a national scale.

Government Structure and Responsibilities

In order to implement this vision, we propose a new structure and outline of duties for a strong, responsive governmental structure that will meet the needs of its citizens at the national (federal) level and provide enough flexibility to create customized solutions at the community level. The modern state was successful in its articulation of important political precepts; the values underlying the federal system, the separation of powers, and the protection of individual rights and liberties are important and should be preserved. The structures that embody these values, however, should be modified to prevent the undue concentration of political and economic resources in the hands of an elite.

All people should have basic human needs secured, all should have equal opportunity for development of their unique human potential, and all should have equal access to participation in community decision making. Individual security and significance and the existence of a healthy community are two sides of the same coin.

To move toward these goals, we make the following specific proposals: 1. a concentration of decision making in community-level governments; 2. the abolition of superfluous intermediary governments (county, state, provincial, district), recognizing that in some countries an intervening unit may be desirable; 3. modifications in the existing institutions of the central or national government; and 4. the creation of a fourth branch for the central government. We believe this basic structure would be viable for countries in different stages of growth and development.

National Government

The main functions of the federal government will be the following:

1. to provide national security and to promote peace and prosperity locally, nationally, and internationally;

2. to set national goals for education and personal welfare and to provide resources to help meet them;
3. to protect individual freedoms and liberties;
4. to facilitate commerce among local communities and to assist the integration of individuals and local businesses in the national and international economies.

These functions will be undertaken by four branches of government: the executive, the legislative, the judicial, and the national wealth trust.

Executive Branch

The executive branch will be headed by the president of the republic, whose duties will include serving as commander-in-chief of all national forces and as head of a national bureau for investigation of human and individual rights, responsible for protecting universal rights against violation by public or private special interests. The president will be elected by direct national suffrage for a five-year term, with a limit of two terms.

Legislative Branch

The legislative branch, charged with making laws for the nation as a whole, will consist of two houses or chambers: the national assembly and the council of the senate. The members of the national assembly, with one representative for every 270,000 citizens, will be elected by direct popular suffrage for three-year terms with a maximum of three terms. Forty of the seventy-one members of the council of the senate will be elected by direct popular suffrage from each of forty separate geographic districts, and must be residents of those districts. The national assembly shall vote the other thirty-one members into office from distinguished representatives of the arts, sciences, agriculture, industry, and commerce, and the general citizenry. They will serve five-year terms, with a two-term limit.

Federal Judicial Branch

The federal judicial branch will be responsible for interpreting and applying constitutional, statutory, and common law. The highest federal court, the supreme court, will consist of nine justices, each with one fifteen-year term. The justices will be nominated by the president of the republic and ratified by majority vote of both chambers of the legislative branch. At the local level, each community will have an independent local court. There will be one district court for every ten local courts.

The National Wealth Trust Branch

We deviate from the structural model of the modern state in calling for a fourth branch of the central government, the national trust branch. This branch will be charged with: 1. management of common lands, air, and other shared community assets; 2. control and management of financial institutions; 3. support for integration of individuals into national and international markets; and 4. financial support and protection of community governments.

The national wealth trust branch of the national government

will generate income by negotiating use permits and collecting entrance fees for the nation's commonly owned land, pastures, parks, historic buildings, and national museums, as well as access to and use of publicly owned airwaves, patents by public universities, and extraction and ownership of mineral resources within public lands. In many countries these public resources are at present controlled by large corporations, which provide little benefit to the general public in return for the resources they extract. The national wealth trust branch will change that by serving as a trustee for all natural resources not currently held as personal property. It also will serve as a repository for national income and other assets.

All funds collected from use permits, entry fees, and fines for abuse of use permits or public property will be placed in a financial institution similar to a national trust for protection and preservation. All funds in the national wealth trust branch shall remain there in perpetuity for use by current and future generations of citizens. This allows for establishment of a venture capital fund that can be used both by individuals, community, and central governments.

Taxes collected by the executive branch of the national government will not be used for any functions carried out by the national wealth trust branch of government. Founds in the position of the national trust fund will also perform like a venture capital fund, providing money for citizens and community governments to foster the development of new technologies created by small, privately owned businesses. The trust's share of profits from new and emerging businesses will become part of the public wealth. The national wealth trust branch will receive a portion of the profit based on agreements with each business that is funded.

When this wealth is publicly owned, it can be reinvested to promote innovation for the public good. Community governments, local communities, private and public institutions, and individuals will be eligible to borrow funds for self, community, or social improvements. National wealth trust branch representatives will review applications for loans and will award monies to be used based on the criteria of level of improvement and contribution to the public good. Monies borrowed under this system will be repaid with a reasonable amount of interest, reflected by current market rates.

We believe the national wealth trust branch to be vitally important in preserving the independence of community government. This new branch of government will also safeguard achievements and help to fulfill a number of collective goals:

1. ensuring the careful management and sustainable use of precious and limited natural resources;
2. encouraging and enabling individual initiative and creativity important to both personal satisfaction and fulfillment by allowing the community government to partner with entrepreneurs in providing the two basic needs of security and significance;
3. encouraging the preservation of local resources;
4. creating vital and viable local communities, which will enjoy reduced crime rates, improved health outcomes, and other benefits;
5. keeping the control and exploitation of limited national resources from the hands of a few large, private corporations that profit at the public expense and have no allegiance to the well-being of the nation or its citizens.

The head of the national wealth trust branch will be elected by direct popular vote. Each candidate will be investigated by the judicial branch before becoming eligible to be placed on the ballot. The term of office will be five years, limited to two terms. This branch of government will be subject to the same philosophy of checks and balances as all other branches of the government. The head of this new branch will be subject to the same impeachment procedures as other elected officials and the entire branch will be subject to an audit once each elected term.

The national wealth trust branch will create departments for each type of resource and funding source listed above, with professional review of loan and use permits. For example, the parks department might make policy decisions about the number of visitors to each park that will maximize citizen visitation without overtaxing natural resources. Perhaps the implementation of a visitor lottery will be necessary for the more popular parks. This could make available for citizens the opportunity to visit the park in their lifetime yet limit them from multiple visits so that other citizens will also have the opportunity to visit. The same detailed attention will be given to oil and natural gas reserves, grazing land, and all the other publicly owned wealth in the country.

The head of each national wealth trust branch department will be elected by direct suffrage for a period of ten years. The judicial branch will investigate all nominees for experience and capability before they are placed on the ballot. Each department will own and manage all national assets and incomes generated within its jurisdiction. These funds will be placed in a national trust fund for protection and preservation in perpetuity.

Local Community Government
(see Figure I at end of chapter)

The primary purpose of local government will be to create a nurturing community environment that promotes human dignity, growth, and prosperity through the following measures:

1. Using per capita funding from the executive branch of the national government for the provision of government services;
2. Preserving the environment for the use and enjoyment of the entire community;
3. Requiring each citizen to work at least one day a month for the community;
4. Building a partnership between individuals and the community to provide resources for the development of individual talents. This will include assessing family or individual needs; developing a long-term plan for property and growth based on these needs, incubating individual talents for infusion of support, and applying for loans from the national trust fund;
5. Supporting individual community-based initiatives for prosperity and growth;
6. Promoting a sense of community pride. All public institutions, hospitals, schools, sport arenas, and parks should be a source of citizen pride;
7. Promoting home ownership or financing housing for all members of the community;
8. Reflecting community values in educational programs by encouraging citizen participation in the educational system.

Each local government will comprise 250,000 to 300,000 people and will be defined by a geographic boundary encompassing a portion of a city or urban area. As communities grow, a new community will be formed to maintain the population ratio.

The executive head of each community government, the governor, will be elected by direct popular suffrage for a five-year term, limited to two terms.

The lieutenant governors, with experience and training in the fields of education, health, housing, entreprencurial development, community security and development, and dispute resolution, will be the cabinet members of the governor. They will be employees of the community government and will be hired for five years, with additional five-year terms dependent on receiving a vote of confidence from the citizens of their community. They are responsible for developing an administrative structure that provides community services through volunteer citizen workers and professionals, freeing financial resources for the improvement of living conditions in the community and fostering a sense of community ownership and pride.

For every 2,500 to 3,000 citizens there will be one social worker. The social worker will act as a citizen advocate and consultant for economic well-being and family development. Social workers will prepare an individualized plan of budgeting and economic success for each family or individual. Based on these budgets and needs, they will provide support and help in contacting the national trust fund for loans. Social workers will use volunteer citizen workers on an as-needed basis according to their expertise. Social workers will be hired for a five-year term, renewable with at least sixty-five percent approval from their constituent base.

Community members will elect one local representative for every 500 citizens. Each local representative will serve as a consultant and assistant to a social worker and as the point of contact for community members. Local representatives will serve as community confidantes and facilitators and will be rewarded through recognition for their community work.

Trust Networks and the Success of Community-Centric Governance

Given the current state of politics in Iran and much of the MENA countries, how might such a new government be created? The issue of how human communities and tribes of people organize and interact has fascinated scholars and writers for decades. While democracy has always been connected to having the consent of the people, there is evidence that having the consent of what Charles Tilly calls trust networks is a paramount, necessary component of not only democracies, but of almost all other forms of government, from dictatorships to oligarchies, theocracies, and monarchies.[2] A trust network is defined as a group of people tied closely together through their beliefs, practices, values, and goals. These connections may be based on religion, tribe, kinship, craft, profession, or a similar long-term vision or goal. Members of a trust network may or may not share a common geographical location.

Trust networks develop through repeated and frequent interpersonal interaction. Membership in a trust network by definition involves acceptance of the risk involved in believing in and depending on other human beings. The risk involved in establishing this level of trust is assumed more easily in smaller groups. In fact, trust networks can help make local governments create conditions conducive to individual development and effective decision making. Trust networks have developed and succeeded both inside and outside official political systems throughout human history, providing benefits and protections for their members while ensuring commonly accepted standards of conduct. As these networks are integrated into public decision making, the government gains the support of the networks and the networks, in turn, become connected to a responsive government.

The future of the truly democratic state will occur in societies connected by a web-like structure of multiple and overlapping trust networks. Although trust networks in themselves do not guarantee the development of true democracy, they are necessary for its existence and its survival. Trust networks support people's willingness to take the risks necessary to make decisions about the values and conditions of the community and the individual. As trust networks multiply, expand, and interweave, the scope of participatory decision-making grows as well. And as participation and cooperation increase, so do security and significance — the basic human needs. Becoming part of a trust network enables humans to fully accept responsibility in creating and sustaining the world in which they live.

Members of a trust network share an obligation, explicit or implied, to help each other and the group. Membership in a trust network includes the possibility of individual or group benefit. It also is possible that some action (or lack of action) by one or more members of the network may harm other members. Therefore, membership in a trust network implies both the opportunity for significant benefit and the risk of significant negative outcomes. As a result, most trust networks enforce standards of conduct for their members. Not every group of people can be called a trust network; some groups are simply social networks. Though members of a social network may help each other, they are not obligated to do so; they may drift into and out of the network in a casual manner, and there are few sanctions for inappropriate actions other than the revocation of membership.

In some cases, especially when severe social or political persecution is present, membership in a trust network may be covert. Members may hold meetings or gatherings until their philosophy either dies out or becomes more mainstream. By upholding standards, including that of secrecy and loyalty, members provide protection to each other and to the group as a whole.

When they are not suppressed or persecuted (and sometimes even when they are), trust networks can help democracy develop and flourish. This is true particularly when such networks operate in collaboration with community governments. The overall population of the community is relatively small, enabling closer connections and easier interaction. The local government becomes a mediator among trust networks, which then learn cooperation rather than hostility in the allocation of resources for community and trust network members. In a developing or established democracy, any number of trust networks may arise, grow, change, and die as they work to build or break down political processes and power structures. Trust networks can be used to enable both individual aspiration and collective growth. In general, this aspiration and growth leads toward more prosperity and greater social cooperation.

Modern democracies are based on a broad "trusting public" that is created from smaller trust networks that support citizen involvement in local and national government. Tilly maintains that such democracies would not have arisen merely from social tolerance and general mutual goals. Instead, their creation depended upon the mutual reliance, duty, and service of people belonging to trust networks. Trust networks not only gave the new democracies cohesion, but having these social structures and personal connections in place allowed newly established governments to work much more effectively.

The idea that a government can use leaders and trust networks to make routine matters of government run smoothly — especially at the community level — is known as noncontentious politics. In many instances, trust networks can help to establish noncontentious politics, in which governments and trust networks cooperate to enhance development and encourage growth. It also is true that governments have persecuted certain trust networks, and that some trust networks have attempted to undermine their own government. If trust networks and government cooperate at the community level and the central government ensures individual human rights, the probability of conflict is reduced. Contentious politics, on the other hand, tends to be more aggressive, sometimes even violent. There is less willingness to incorporate "outsiders" into the political system, less tolerance for diversity of opinion, and a less equitable distribution of power.

Trust networks have flourished both inside and outside of official political processes and structures for thousands of years, providing benefits and protections and enforcing standards of conduct for their members. When they are integrated into public politics in a noncontentious way through broadened participation and cross-consultations between the government and the networks, the government becomes both more effective and more responsive to the needs of the people. In sum, both the past and the future of democracy depend on a web of connection across trust networks, social networks, and community and national government.

Trust Networks, Bargaining, and the Creation of Democracy

Trust networks are involved in the bargaining processes within a given political system. It is this interaction that results in the creation of government policies. Bargaining can occur among citizens, trust networks, other social groups, government institutions,[3] and governments themselves. The transition to democracy begins with bargaining, which is a predecessor to civil society and rule of law. If successful, the process of bargaining strengthens the connection of people to their government. Bargaining is a crucial collective-choice process by which demands and claims are adjudicated and community actors learn trust in the process.

It is not necessary for the masses to demand democracy for it to occur. In the development of modern democracies, as Tilley points out, "few if any of the participants were self-consciously trying to create democratic institutions . . . *In watching democratization, we witness an erratic, improvisational, struggle-ridden process in which continuities and cumulative effects arise more from constraints set by widely shared but implicit understandings and existing social relations than from any clairvoyant vision of the future."[4]* In short, democracy is often the unintended — and for some unwanted — consequence of political struggle within the community, rather than the intended result of a bargaining process. Since democracy often emerges from passionate political struggles, it can be unstable and not well defined, as is evident in such places as Egypt, where people currently working in governmental positions are falling back on the old regime's rules. This exemplifies what Tilley identifies as de-democratization. It also highlights the difference between a trust network and other social groups. The population group that demonstrated successfully in Egypt had no internal standards, no cohesive values, no mutual trust, no sanctions that could be placed on a member of the group who did not act in accord with its goals.

Tilly warns that any existing democracy will face de-democratization if the only support is a single trust network, as is the case in Egypt with the popular confrontation between Ikhwanul Muslimin (the Muslim Brotherhood) and the other social groups. A democracy cannot tolerate deception by a trust network in power. Non-transparency and de-democratization will cause the loss of support of its citizens, who then will withdraw their resources, including funds, labor, intellectual support, and natural resources. Trust networks may revert to underground activities, and their leaders may try to hold things together by using force, which causes the democracy to dissolve. Discourse becomes more ideological, and the ability to cooperate to solve problems is weakened. If the political system does not return to equilibrium, the smooth operation of democracy may be threatened. These disruptions in the early stages of democratization are perhaps unavoidable. For this reason it may be best to begin experiments in democracy at the level of community government, where the early turbulence can be more easily sustained, until bargaining becomes an accepted part of the political process.

In order to create governmental change, trust networks must integrate themselves into the community's political process. Brokered autonomy is often a first step in this integration. Suppressed tribes or other groups may be given autonomy, which causes a cessation of hostility. Eventually these tribes may be integrated into the larger citizen body. Trust groups in power may offer concessions, including resources and an end to antigovernment action, in return for a share of government power. This is possible only in small community governments. As the relationship between the government and a trust network grows, integration and mutual dependence develop. Trust networks gain a stake in government and have a reason for maintaining stability and working within the political system for change and betterment. The interests and strategies of trust networks become the engines of social and political change.

Continuing alterations in power configurations — both within community governments and outside of them — mark the process of democratization. Although infrequent, democratization sometimes even occurs "at the initiative of power holders attempting to maintain their power." Dominant elites more frequently reject power-sharing claims and demands from trust networks and other social groups. In a well-functioning community government, strong, farsighted, dedicated, and cohesive trust networks can effectively counter the positions of the elite. Elite consent is not a precondition for the building of democratic process within the small community; trust network involvement is. A popular political struggle coupled with solid trust networks can promote the integration of these trust networks into a new public political structure. In such structures, the power of autonomous elites or structures may be subordinated, and power may be distributed more broadly, creating a mutually binding citizen-state collaboration.

This collaboration provides benefits both upstream and downstream, creating a dynamic and flexible government structure that better serves the population. It also creates citizen "buy-in" regarding the legitimacy of their local government. When this happens, there is reduction in central government control by armed forces and violence. Competition for resources among local community governments will lead to a reduction of categorical inequality in public politics. External guarantees develop, and mutual dependence grows, and government capacity expands. "In the long run, increases in governmental capacity and protected consultation reinforce each other; as government expansion generates resistance, bargaining, and provisional settlements, on one side, while on the other side protected consultation encourages demands for expansion of government intervention, which promote increases in capacity . . . If ample governmental capacity does not define democracy, it looks like a nearly necessary condition for democracy on a large scale."[5]

Civil society is based on a social contract dependent on a level of trust within a community. The trust that exists in trust networks is the basis of a larger social trust that emerges from the political process of community governments. The social trust that flows from increased interaction and bargaining in the political arena binds citizens together in recognition of their mutual interdependence and in their pursuit of individual and group values and interests. Only then can a truly democratic state be realized.

An Unprecedented Opportunity

The fundamental sociopolitical changes sweeping the Middle East and North Africa provide an unprecedented opportunity for humanity to experiment with more effective and participatory forms of democracy. In fact, the freedom and support offered by such a government played a critical role in the dramatic creative and economic growth during Iran's Golden Age.

Now, these communities can serve as the nexus for a true participatory democracy that generates individual and communal creativity, growth and prosperity. The community-centric governance model proposed here offers a powerful alternative to the liberal democratic model of special-interest-driven representative democracy. In the community-centric model, local governments provide all direct governmental services that are local in nature. The community-centric governance model is much more compatible with the MENA region's rich urban history, natural geography, and current sociopolitical realities. Rather than a poor imitation and adaptation of an existing Western form of governance, it builds on the communitarian culture of the region.

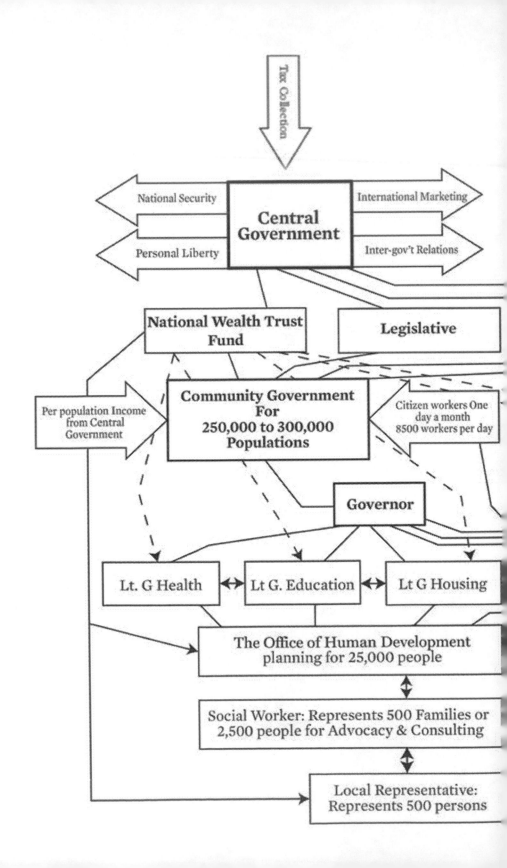

FIGURE 1

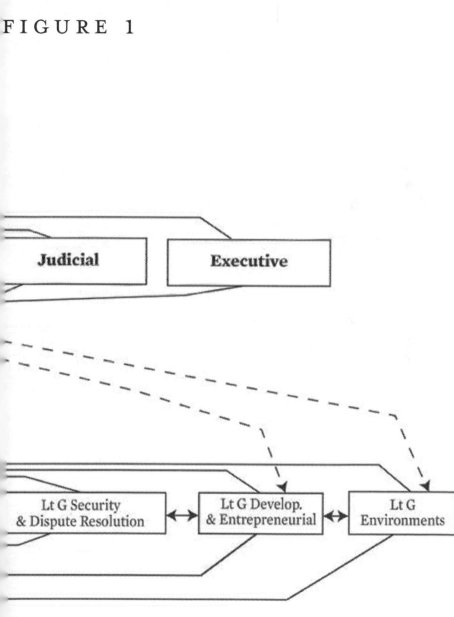

CONCLUSION

The evolution of governmental models from ancient to modern times is the result of human innovation in the art of community-building. Changes in the models have had very great consequences on the sociopolitical development of humanity, yet significant changes are difficult to achieve, and over thousands of years of civilization, those changes have been relatively few. For centuries, successful communities saw no reason to accept any fundamental changes in the political order of their states.

In fact, from the Bronze Age to modern times, we can only identify three major models for governmental structure: monarchic or absolute rule, multicultural empires, and the modern state, which features a separation of powers and a national rule of law. The unfortunate truth is this: Social upheavals, and even so-called "revolutions" based on demands for an improved social order, usually result in governmental structures and socioeconomic realities that closely resemble the past political order and fail to bring about the desired social change.

The absolute rulers of the past, from the Bronze Age onward for thousands of years, had a simple objective: assimilating or annihilating all communities at their borders and imposing their culture on the territories they conquered. About 2,500 years ago, the appearance of imperial political order caused a fundamental shift in this approach. Forward-thinking leaders, starting with Cyrus the Great, began to understand the possibility of building political structures that governed many diverse human communities.

This imperial model had a lasting impact on human understanding of politics and socioeconomic growth. It also represents a pivotal point in human political history and a new threshold in human development: the tolerance of diversity. Cyrus the Great imagined this first historical change in governance in the fifth century BCE. He and Darius the Great established the first imperial state, which tolerated other nations' religious and cultural ideals in return for their economic and political cooperation. Their efforts would have far-reaching consequences.

In Iran, this novel form of governance created the largest diversified human community to that date and caused growth, innovation, and a dramatic flowering of culture within the empire. This new form of government spread eastward to the Qin dynasty in China and westward to Rome, influencing the Roman Empire to build a similar political structure. Later, the British Empire would follow suit. The political systems of these multicultural empires were notable for their tolerance of the religions and cultures of colonized peoples. In short, tolerance for national self-expression was a simple innovation that enabled the formation of these large political entities, which have made numerous contributions to the growth of humanity for over two thousand years.

In the eighteenth century, the British colonies in America, which had been established by Europeans who escaped religious persecution in their own countries, gained freedom from the British Empire and established the foundation of the modern state. Because of their historical roots in religious persecution in Europe and their colonial status, the idea of a tolerant state and the freedom of religion appealed to the founders of the United States. The modern state they created extended these values to individuals, casting aside the idea of citizens as subjects of an empire and creating free citizens with inalienable rights who controlled the destiny of their own government. This represents the second significant shift in the governmental model. The citizens of this new republic, with protected rights and freedom, built the mightiest state in world history in less than 150 years, an unprecedented achievement.

At the time of Cyrus's rule, Persia was a small and insignificant state far from the main powerful contenders. Yet by using tolerance and cooperation as the primary basis for empire building, he and Darius managed to build the world's largest empire based on a collective of cooperating communities within a single state structure. The Founding Fathers of the United States followed Cyrus's pattern of tolerance in formulating the Constitution by putting a free citizenry and the tolerance of others' rights and beliefs at the center of the new republic. In a relatively short period of time, these principles turned a remote colonial outpost into a mighty civilization.

Yet history has shown that human capacity to understand, as well as our expectations of government, constantly change. As a result, the old social structure will eventually have to be replaced. In the case of the modern state, the corrupting influence of powerful corporations has rendered democracy ineffective. There is need for a new model, yet this model will likely not come from the most powerful of the modern states. In fact, it is noteworthy that established, powerful political entities have seldom experimented with meaningful social change. There is a simple reason for this: Such experimentation could result in the relocation of power, and those who wield great power seldom surrender it voluntarily. For this reason, nascent states with a lesser degree of organization and a less-established power structure have often served as the laboratories for the development of new political models.

The rise of global culture and technology has created more possibility than ever for the individual to have positive impact upon society. For this reason, the new social order will likely be based on models that allow much greater numbers of citizens to be empowered, to use innovations in solving problems, and to practice their creativity for the benefit of humankind. History has also demonstrated that any small and insignificant country that solves constraining social problems will not remain small and insignificant for long. The most important components of change are simple: tolerance of diversity and trust of the community of free citizens nourished by local incubators for development of creativity of individuals. The potential for such an arrangement exists in many nations, and those that take the opportunity will earn the rewards. States that currently hold little power may well wield great power in the future.

The model of government that we have proposed in this book is, clearly, a simple evolution of the existing modern state. We believe that momentum is gathering for another paradigm shift in governance, one in which free individual citizens are trusted and empowered to develop their full potential growth and prosperity and receive full support for their needs as community members.

The adoption of our model will create communities in which government presents fewer bureaucratic and social obstacles for actualizing people's creativity and desires. These communities will be organized around a common set of simple ideas and principles, and individual diversity will be tolerated and celebrated. Empowered local citizens will be in charge of creating responsive, locally based governments and economies, in contrast to the current, highly centralized modern state that controls all resources from a distance and must suppress diversity and individual creativity in order to retain control.

If applied, the simple changes we have proposed can become powerful weapons for creating strong, resourceful, and powerful states. Sooner or later there will be a successor to the modern state. Most likely, this new model will emerge from a dynamic society with the capacity to empower its creative citizens, and become a dominant social and cultural force in the future. Iran and the nations of MENA, should they choose it, can lead the way.

NOTES

INTRODUCTION

No notes.

PREFACE

Ian Morris Why the West Rules — for Now: The Pattern of History and What They Reveal About The Future (New York: Farrar, Straus and Giroux New York 2010).

CHAPTER 1

1. The social history of Iran contains many dark periods. The research for this chapter was done as a separate work on the social history of Iran, which will be published later. We have decided to refrain from providing the source material for our historical observations, which come from primary and original sources that will not add to the focus of this work.

2. Edward Said, Orientalism (New York: Vintage Books 1979).

3. General Sir Percy Molesworth Sykes trans. by M.T Daghi Gilani Donya e Ketab The History of Persia (Tehran: Elmi 1988).

CHAPTER 2

1. The analysis in this section is indebted to Lynn H. Nelson, "The Impact of Discovery on Europe," World History Syllabus (Lawrence, Kansas:

University of Kansas Department of History, February 26, 1968, http://vlib.iue.it/carrie/reference/worldhistory/sections/19impact.html.

2. Max Weber, *Economy and Society* (Berkeley: University of California Press, 1978).

3. Christopher Pierson, *The Modern State* (London: Routledge, 1996), http://psi424.cankaya.edu.tr/uploads/files/Pierson,%20The%20Modern%20State,%202nd%20ed.PDF.

4. Harold Laski, *Authority in the Modern State* (New Haven: Yale University Press, 1919), reprinted by Batoche Books, Kitchener, Ontario, 2000.

5. Hilton L. Root, *The Fountain of Privilege: Political Foundations of Markets in Old Regime France and England* (Berkeley: University of California Press, 1994), http://ark.cdlib.org/ark:/13000030/ft1779n74g/.

6. Karl Polanyi, *The Great Transformation: The Political and Economic Origins of Our Times* (Boston: Beacon Press, 2001).

7. Ibid, 38.

8. Ibid, 39.

9. Robert L. Heilbroner, *The Worldly Philosophers* (New York: Simon and Schuster, 1953), 19.

10. Montesquieu, *The Spirit of the Laws,* trans. T. Nugent, rev. J.V. Pritchard (London: G. Bell & Sons, 1949).

11. Ibid, Book II, Sec. 2.

12. Ibid, Book XI, Sec. 6.

13. Ibid, Book IX, Sec 6

14. The legislative power enacts laws, the executive power is that which "makes peace or war, sends or receives embassies, establishes the public security, and provides against invasions" and the judiciary is a special type of executive power concerned with civil disputes and criminal punishment. "There would be an end to everything, were the same man or the same body, whether of the nobles or of the people, to exercise those three powers, that of enacting laws, that of executing the public resolutions, and of trying the causes of individuals" (From Ibid, Book IX, Sec. 6).

15. Ibid, Sec. 6.

16. Ibid, Sec. 6.

17. Ibid, Sec. 6.

18. Karl Marx, *Manifesto of the Communist Party* (1848), http://www.marx.org/Archive/1848-CM, 2.

19. Ibid.

20. Murray Forsyth, "Alexander Hamilton, John Jay, and James Madison: The Federalist," *The Political Classics: Hamilton to Mill,* ed. M. Forsyth, M. Keens-Soper, and J. Hoffman (New York: Oxford University Press, 1993), 36-37.

21. Ibid, 36-37.

22. This provision was later changed to allow direct election of Senators.

23. There was yet another issue to consider in determining the proportion of representatives allotted to each state: Should slaves be counted and, if so, how? Clearly, they were not citizens and were not granted the right of suffrage. The issue was solved by agreeing to count each slave as three-fifths of a person in the allotment of representatives. This system of "counting"

was nullified by the passage of the Thirteenth Amendment abolishing slavery.

24. The body comprises delegates from each state equivalent to its combined number of senators and Representatives and chosen by each state legislature. In the event no candidate received a majority of the votes, the House received the right to choose the chief executive. In the event no candidate received a majority of the votes, the House received the right to choose the chief executive. While still formally in effect, electors from each state cast their votes in accord with that state's popular vote. The question of whether or not to abolish the Electoral College continues to be debated.

25. Forsyth, "Hamilton, Jay, and Madison," 17.

26. This also requires a two-thirds vote of both houses of Congress.

27. As pointed out, the Bill of Rights as originally implemented applied only to citizens in their relationship with the federal government. Over time, the Supreme Court, using the equal protection clause of the Fourteenth Amendment as a foundation, gradually "incorporated" many of these rights to apply to citizens in their relationship with state governments as well. This process continued into the late 1960s.

28. This is, of course, a gross oversimplification of the complex and sometime conflicting arguments presented by Locke and Rousseau.

29. Daniel D. Rodgers, "Rights Consciousness in American History," *The Bill of Rights in American History*, ed. D.J. Brodenhemer and J. W. Ely (Bloomington: Indiana University Press, 2008), 13-14.

30. The Thirteenth Amendment was ratified in 1865. The Fourteenth Amendment (1868) contains, among other provisions, this crucial statement: No state "shall make or enforce any law which shall abridge the privileges or immunities of citizens of the United States; nor shall any State deprive any person of life, liberty, or property, without due process of law;

nor deny to any person within its jurisdiction the equal protection of the law." The Fifteenth Amendment (1870) provides that the "right of citizens of the United States to vote shall not be denied or abridged by the United States or by any State on account of race, color, or previous condition of servitude" and that the "Congress shall have power to enforce this article by appropriate legislation." Women were given the right to vote by the Nineteenth Amendment (1920).

31. Rodgers, "Rights Consciousness," 14.

32. Rodgers, "Rights Consciousness," 9.

33. Rodgers, "Rights Consciousness," 16-17.

34. The Court ruled, for example, that a privately owned motel located on an interstate highway or a restaurant that bought supplies from another state were engaged in interstate commerce, an activity whose regulation was given to Congress in Article III of the Constitution. Combined with the portion of the Fourteenth Amendment that provides for "equal protection" of all citizens, the federal government was thus able to overturn state laws that allowed for segregation or discrimination in the private sector.

35. Until the Court ruled in 1966 (*Griswold v. Connecticut*) that it constituted an unlawful intrusion of the state into an area of life in which there was a reasonable expectation of privacy, Connecticut prohibited the sale of any contraceptives, even to married couples.

36. A glaring exception to this is the wholesale denial of rights, loss of property, and forced, involuntary internment in relocation camps of over 100,000 people of Japanese ancestry (two-thirds of whom were United States citizens) between 1942 and 1945. The internment, carried out under an executive order of President Roosevelt, was aimed primarily at residents of the Pacific Coast, although other areas were affected as well. Those selected to go to the armed and secured "relocation camps," which were characterized by inadequate shelter, sanitation, and cooking facilities,

were removed from their homes with little prior notice, often being able to take only the clothes on their backs.

CHAPTER 3

1. Richard N. Cooper, "Problems with the Protocol," Harvard Magazine (2002), http://harvardmagazine.com/2002/11 problems-with-the-protocol.

2. Jess M. Krannich, "The Corporate 'Person': A New Analytical Approach to a Flawed Method of Constitutional Interpretation," Loyola University Chicago Law Journal 37 (2005), 67-68.

3. Ibid, "70.

4. Ibid, "77.

5. Ibid, 77.

6. Adolph Berle and Gardiner Means, The Modern Corporation and Private Property (New York: Harcourt Brace, rev. ed, 1968).

7. Adam Liptak, "Corporate Cash Floods U.S. Elections," Chicago Tribune (January 22, 2010), http://www.commondreams.org/headline/2010/08/02-0."

8. Ibid.

9. Tom Hamburger, "Justices, 5-4, Reject Corporate Spending Limit," The New York Times (August 2, 2010), http://www.nytimes.com/2010/01/22/us/politics/22.

10. Sarah Anderson and John Cavanagh, Top 200: The Rise of Corporate Global Power (Washington, D.C.: Institute for Policy Studies, 2000), 1.

11. Adam Tokar, "Something Happened: Sovereignty and European Integration," IWM Junior Visiting Fellows Conference 11 (Vienna, 2001).

12. Ibid.

13. Ibid.

14. Alain Pellet, "State Sovereignty and the Protection of Fundamental Human Rights: An International Perspective," Pugwash Occasional Papers 2 (2000), 37-45.

15. Thomas L. Friedman, The World is Flat: A Brief History of the Twenty-First Century, interviewed by Joanne J. Myers (Carnegie Council, 2005), http://www.cceia.org/resources/transcripts/5134.

16. David M. Kotz, "The Financial and Economic Crisis of Neoliberal Capitalism," Review of Radical Political Economics 41 (2009), 307.

17. Ibid, 306.

18. Ibid.

19. Ibid, 308-309.

20. Ibid, 312.

21. Jacob S. Hacker and Paul Pierson, Winner-Take-All Politics (New York: Simon and Schuster, 2010), 290.

22. Jacob S. Hacker, "Technology and Current Affairs," interviewed by Charlie Rose, National Public Radio (October 25, 2010).

23. Thomas S. Kuhn, The Structure of Scientific Revolutions (Chicago: University of Chicago Press, 1962), 74-84.

24. Cooper, "Problems with the Protocol."

25. Cooper, "Problems with the Protocol."

26. Guy Raz, "Defining the War on Terror," National Public Radio, *All Things Considered* (November 1, 2006).

27. Tokar, "Something Happened."

28. Kuhn, The Structure of Scientific Revolutions, 29.

29. Ibid, 92.

30. Maury Klein, "The Technological Revolution," Foreign Policy Research Institute 13 (2008), http:www.fpri.org/articles/2008/07technologicalrevol ution, 5- 6.

31. The phrase is from Shakespeare's "The Tempest," Act 5, Scene 1, and is also the title of Aldous Huxley's dystopian novel.

32. Klein, "Technological Revolution," 5-6.

33. This part of Schumpeter's analysis is taken from two works: Joseph A. Schumpeter, "The Instability of Capitalism," The Economic Journal 38 (1928), 361-386, http://www.jstor.org/stable/2224315, and Joseph A. Schumpeter, *The Theory of Economic Development,* trans. Redvers Opies (New Brunswick: Transaction Publishers, 1934).

34. Gerhard Fischer, Elisa Giaccaardi, Hal Eden, Masanori Sugimot, and Yunwen Ye, "Beyond Binary Choices: Integrating Individual and Social Creativity." International Journal of Human-Computer Studies 63 (2005), 482, www.elservier.com/locate/ijhes.

35. Roger Wettenhall, "Civic Engagement, Decentralization and Local Democracy: Some Questions and Issues," paper for World Civic Forum (Seoul, South Korea, 2009), http://unpan/.un.org/intradoc/grooups/ public/documents/un- dpadm/unpan039945.

36. Anthony Giddens, The Third Way and Its Critics (Oxford: Polity Press, 2000.)

37. Herbert Werlin, "The Community: Master or Client? — A Review of the Literature," Public Administration and Development 4 (1989), 447-457.

CHAPTER FOUR

1. Alfarabi, The Political Writings: "Selected Aphorism" and Other Texts, trans. and annot. Charles E. Butterfield (Ithaca: Cornell University Press, 2001).

2. Charles Tilley, *Democracy* (New York: Cambridge University Press, 2007).

3. Charles Tilley, *Trust and Rule* (New York: Cambridge University Press, 2005), 33.

4. Ibid, 100.

5. Ibid, 100-149.

BIBLIOGRAPHY

Persian History References

Balghami. *Tarikh nameh Tabari*. Vols. 1, 2, and 3. Tehran: M. Roushan Nasher Alborz, 1373.

Balkhi, Mohamad ibn Khavand Shah. *Rouzeh al Safa*. Vols. 1 and 2. Translated by A. Zaryab. Tehran: Entesharat Elmi, 1373.

Boyce, Mary. *A History of Zoroastrianism*. Vol. 1, *The Early Period*. Translated by Homayoon San'ati'zadeh. Tehran: Entesharat Tus, 1375.

Collins, Robert. *The Medes and Persians: Conquerors and Diplomats*. New York: McGraw-Hill Books, 1975

Dabire, Khajeh A. Mohammad Ibn Housien Bayhaghi. *Tarikh Bayhaghi*. Edited by Khatib Rahbar. Tehran: Mehtab, 1371.

Froozonfar, Badegh al Zamon. *Sokhan va Sokhanvaron*. Tehran: Entesharat Kharazmi, 1358.

Ghishmam, R. *Iran*. New York: Penguin Books, 1961.

Ibn-Yaghoub, Ahmad. *Tarikh Yaghoubi*. 2nd ed., vols. 1 and 2. Translated by M. A. Ayatey. Tehran: Sherkate Entesharat Elmi & Farhangi, 1371.

Jafri, S. Housin M. *The Origins and Early Development of Shi'a Islam*. London: Longman, 1979.

Kadkani, M.R. Shafi. *Ghalandarih Dar Tarikh*. Tehran: Entesharat So'khan, 1386.

Khajeh Nizam al-Mulk. *Siyar al-Muluk* aka *Siyasat Nameh*. Edited by

Hubert Drake. Tehran: Scientific & Cultural Publishing Co., 1372.

Koufi, Mohammad Ibn Ali Ibn Aethem. *Al Foutouh*. Translated by M. A. Moustoufi Heravi. Tehran: Entesharat Amouzesh Inghelab Islami, 1372.

Marrvi, Nasser Khosrow Ghobadiani. *Safer Nameh*. Edited by Dr. M. Dabiersyaghi. Tehran: Entesharat Zavouar, 1373.

Maseudi, Abu Hasan Ali ibn Housien. *Morouj Al Zahab*. Vols. 1 and 2. Translated by Abdul Ghasem Payandeh. Tehran: Entesharat Tus, 1344.

Minavi, Mojtaba. *Farhang va Tariekh*. Tehran: Entesharat Kharazmi, 1369.

———. *Naghed e Hall*. Tehran: Entesharat Kharazmi, 1367.

Mohseni, Housin, and M. J. Sarughadi. *The Meds, Achaemenian and Sasanian*. Tehran: Komruni, 1373.

Pirnia, Hassan. *Darious the Great and Xerxes*. Iran Boston Series. Tehran: Inbe Sina, 1344.

Hamedani, Rashid eddin Fazelalah. *Jameh Al-Tavarikh*. Edited by M. Roushan, M Moussavi. Tehran: Nasher e Alberooz, 1373.

Shaban, M.A. *Islamic History: A new interpretation*. Vol. 1. Cambridge: Cambridge University Press, 1971.

———. *Islamic History: A new interpretation*. Vol. 2. Cambridge: Cambridge University Press, 1976.

———. *The Abbasid Revolution*. Cambridge: Cambridge University Press, 1970.

Tabari, Mohammad ibn-Jarier. *Tarikh Tabari*. Vols. 1-17. Translated by Abdul Ghassem Payandeh. Tehran: Entesharat Assatear, 1372.

Tabatabaei, Seyd Javad. *Khujeh Nezam-ul Molk*. Tehran: Tarhe Nu, 1375.

Youssefi, Ghalam Housien. *Farhang va Tariekh*. Tehran: Entesharat So'khan, 1371

Zarkoob, Dr. Abdul Housien. *Two Centuries of Silence*. Tehran: Katab Khaneh Meli Iran, 1378.

English References

Anderson, Sarah, and John Cavanagh. *Top 200: The Rise of Corporate Global Power*. Washington, D.C.: Institute for Policy Studies, 2000.

Berle, Adolph, and Gardiner Means. *The Modern Corporation and Private Property.* Revised edition. New York: Harcourt Brace, 1968.

Boyce, Mary. *A History of Zoroastrianism,* Vol. 1, *The Early Period.* Translated by Homayoon San'ati'zadeh. Tehran: Entesharat Tus, 1375.

Brodenhemer, David J., and James W. Ely, eds. *The Bill of Rights in Modern America.* Bloomington: Indiana University Press, 2008.

Collins, Robert. *The Medes and the Persians: Conquerors and Diplomats.* New York: McGraw-Hill Books, 1961.

Cooper, Richard N., cited in "Problems with the Protocol." Harvard Magazine, November-December 2002, http://harvardmagazine. com/2002/11/problems-with-the-protoc.

Economist, http://www.economist.com/research/economics/ SearchActionTerms.

Fischer, Gerhard, Elisa Giaccaardi, Hal Eden, Masanori Sugimot, and Yunwen Ye. "Beyond Binary Choices: Integrating Individual and Social Creativity." *International Journal of Human-Computer Studies* 63 (2005): 482-512, www.elsevier.com/locate/ijhes.

Forstater, Mathew. "Visions and Scenarios: Heilbroner's Worldly Philosophy, Lowe's Political Economics, and the Methodology of Ecological Economics." Working Paper 413. Kansas City: The Levy Economics Institute of Bard College, University of Missouri, 2004.

Forsyth, Murray. "Alexander Hamilton, John Jay, and James Madison: The Federalist." In *The Political Classics: Hamilton to Mill.* Edited by M. Forsyth, M. Keens-Soper, and J. Hoffman. New York: Oxford University Press, 1993.

Friedman, Thomas L. *The World is Flat: A Brief History of the Twenty-First Century.* Interviewed by Joanne J. Myers, Carnegie Council, 2005. http://www.cceia.org/resources/transcripts/5134.

Ghishmam, R. *Iran.* New York: Penguin Books, 1961.

Giddens, Anthony. *The Third Way and Its Critics.* Oxford: Polity Press, 2000.

Guehenno, Jean-Marie. *The End of the Nation State.* Translated by Victoria Elliott. Minneapolis: University of Minnesota Press, 2000.

Habermas, Jurgen. *Knowledge and Human Interests.* Boston: Beacon Press, 1975.

Hacker, Jacob. "Technology and Current Affairs." Interviewed by Charlie Rose. National Public Radio, October 25, 2010.

Hacker, Jacob S., and Paul Pierson. *Winner-Take-All Politics*. New York: Simon and Schuster, 2010.

Hamburger, Tom. "Justices, 5-4, Reject Corporate Spending Limit." *The New York Times*, August 2, 2010, http://www.nytimes.com/2010/01/22/us/politics/22scotus.html.

Heilbroner, Robert L. *The Worldly Philosophers*. New York: Simon and Schuster, 1953.

Huffington, Arianna. *Third World America: How Our Politicians are Abandoning the Middle Class and Betraying the American Dream*. New York: Random House, 2011.

Klein, Maury. "The Technological Revolution." Foreign Policy Research Institute 13 (2008), http://www.fpri.org/articles/2008/07/technologicalrevolution.

Kotz, David M. "The Financial and Economic Crisis of Neoliberal Capitalism." *Review of Radical Political Economics* 41 (2009): 305-317, http://rp.sagepub.com/content/41/3/305.

Krannich, Jess M. "The Corporate 'Person': A New Analytical Approach to a Flawed Method of Constitutional Interpretation." *Loyola University Chicago Law Journal* 37 (2005): 61-109.

Kuhn, Thomas S. *The Structure of Scientific Revolutions*. Chicago: University of Chicago Press, 1962.

Lasky, Harold. *Authority in the Modern State*. Kitchener, ON: Batoche Books, 2000.

Lewis-Beck, Michael S. and Mary Stegmaier. "Economic Determinants of Electoral Outcomes." *Annual Review of Political Science* 3 (2000): 18-21.

Liptak, Adam. "Corporate Campaign Cash Floods U.S. Elections." *Chicago Tribune*, January 22, 2010, http://www.commondreams.org/headline/2010/08/02-0.

Locke, John. *Two Treatises of Government*. Edited by T.L. Cook. New York: Hafner Publishing Company, 1966.

Losco, Joseph and Leonard Williams, eds. *Political Theory: Classic Writings, Contemporary Views*. New York: St. Martin's Press, 1992.

Marx, Karl. *Manifesto of the Communist Party*, 1848, http://www.marx. org/Archive/1848-CM.

Maslow, Abraham. *A Theory of Human Motivation*. New York: Harper, 1954.

Max-Neef, Manfred A. *Human Scale Development: Conception, Application and Further Reflections*. New York: Apex, 1991.

Montesquieu, Charles de Secondat. *The Spirit of Laws*, 1752. Translated by T. Nugent. Revised by J.V. Prichard. London: G. Bell & Sons, 1914.

Osbun, Lee Ann. *The Problem of Participation*. New York: University Press of America, 1985.

Pellet, Alain. "State Sovereignty and the Protection of Fundamental Human Rights: An International Perspective." *Pugwash Occasional Papers* 1 (2000): 37-45.

Perez, Carlotta. "The Advance of Technology and Major Bubble Collapses: Historical Regulations and Lessons for Today." Engelsberg Seminar on The Future of Capitalism. Axson Foundation, Sweden (June 2010), www.carlottaperez.com.

Polanyi, Karl. *The Great Transformation: The Political and Economic Origins of Our Time*. Boston: Beacon Press, 2001.

Raz, Guy. "Defining the War on Terror." National Public Radio, *All Things Considered*, November 1, 2006.

Rodgers, Daniel D. "Rights Consciousness in American History." In *The Bill of Rights in Modern America*. Edited by D.J. Brodenhemer and J.W. Ely. Bloomington: Indiana University Press, 2008.

Root, Hilton L. *The Fountain of Privilege: Political Foundations of Markets in Old Regime France and England*. Berkeley: University of California Press, 1994, http://ark.cdlib.org/ark:/13000030/ft1779n74g/.

Rousseau, Jean Jacques. *The Social Contract and Discourses*. Translated by G.D.H. Cole. New York: Hafner Publishing Company, 1950.

Schumacher, E.F. *Small is Beautiful: Economics as if People Mattered*. New York: Harper Perennial, 1989.

Schumpeter, Joseph A. "The Instability of Capitalism." *The Economic Journal* 38 (1928): 361-386, http://www.jstor.org/stable/2224315.

Schumpeter, Joseph A. *The Theory of Economic Development: An Inquiry into Profits, Capital, Credit, Interest, and the Business Cycle*. Translated from the German by Redvers Opie. New Brunswick (USA) and London (UK): Transaction Publishers, 1934.

Tilley, Charles. *Democracy.* Cambridge: Cambridge University Press, 2007.

————. *Trust and Rule.* Cambridge: Cambridge University Press, 2005.

Tokar, Adrian. "Something Happened. Sovereignty and European Integration." Extraordinary Times, IWM Junior Visiting Fellows Conference 11, Vienna, 2001.

The U.S. National Archives & Records Administration (NARA). "The Constitution of the United States: A History," 2010, http://www. archives.gov.

Weber, Max. *Economy and Society.* University of California Press, 1978.

Werlin, Herbert. "The Community: Master or Client? — A Review of the Literature." *Public Administration and Development* 4 (1989): 447-457.

Wettenhall, Roger. "Civic Engagement, Decentralization and Local Democracy: Some Questions and Issues." Paper for World Civic Forum, Seoul, South Korea, 2009, http://unpan/.un.org/intradoc/groups/public/documents/un-dpadm/unpan039945.

APPENDIX

Darius was buried at <u>Naqš-i Rustam</u>, where he left two inscriptions

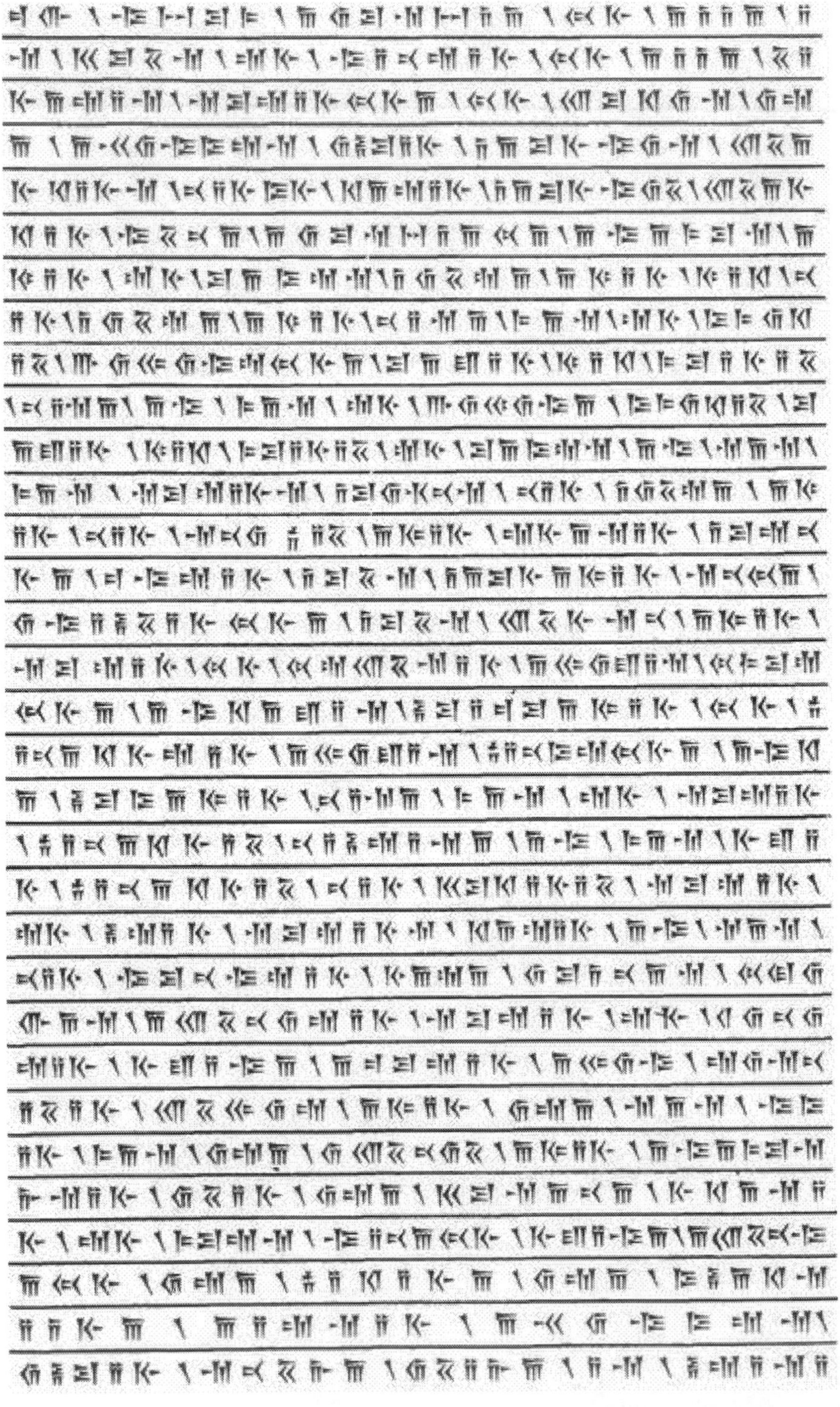

1. baga \ vazraka \ Auramazdâ \ hya \ adadâ \ i
2. ma \ frašam \ tya \ vainataiy \ hya \ adadâ \ ši
3. yâtim \ martiyahyâ \ hya \ xrathum \ ut
4. â \ aruvastam \ upariy \ Dârayavaum \ xšâ
5. yathiyam \ nîyasaya \ thâtiy \ Dârayavauš \ xšâya
6. thiya \ vašnâ \ Auramazdâha \ avâkaram \ a
7. miy \ tya \ râstam \ dauštâ \ amiy \ mitha \ na
8. iy \ dauštâ \ amiy \ naimâ \ kâma \ tya \ skauth
9. iš \ tunuvatahyâ \ râdiy \ mitha \ kariyaiš
10. \ naimâ \ ava \ kâma \ tya \ tunuvâ \ skauthaiš \ r
11. âdiy \ mitha \ kariyaiš \ tya \ râstam \ ava \ mâm \
12. kâma \ martiyam \ draujanam \ naiy \ dauštâ \ am
13. iy \ naiy \ manauviš \ amiy \ tyâmaiy \ dartana
14. yâ \ bavatiy \ daršam \ dârayâmiy \ manahâ \
15. uvaipašiyahyâ \ daršam \ xšayamna \ amiy \
16. martiya \ hya \ hataxšataiy \ anudim \ hakarta
17. hyâ \ avathâdim \ paribarâmiy \ hya \ v
18. inâithayatiy \ anudim \ vinastahyâ \ avath
19. â \ parsâmiy \ naimâ \ kâma \ tya \ martiya
20. \ vinâthayais \ naipatimâ \ ava \ kâma \ yadi
21. y \ vinâthayaiš \ naiy \ frathiyaiš \ martiya \
22. tya \ patiy \ martiyam \ thâtiy \ ava \ mâm \
23. naiy \ varnavataiy \ yâtâ \ uradanâm \ hadu
24. gâm \ âxšnautiy \ martiya \ tya \ kunau
25. tiy \ yadivâ \ âbaratiy \ anuv \ tauman
26. išaiy \ xšnuta \ amiy \ utâ \ mâm \ vas
27. iy \ kâma \ utâ \ uxšnauš \ amiy \ avâkaram
28. camaiy \ ušîy \ utâ \ framânâ \ yathâmai
29. y \ tya \ kartam \ vainâhy \ yadivâ \ âxšnav
30. âhy \ utâ \ vithiyâ \ uta \ spâthma
31. idayâ \ aitamaiy \ aruvastam \
32. upariy \ manašcâ \ ušîcâ \ ima \ patimai

A great god is Ahuramazda, who created this excellent thing which is seen, who created happiness for man, who set wisdom and capability down upon King Darius.

King Darius says: By the grace of Ahuramazda I am of such a sort, I am a friend of the right, of wrong I am not a friend. It is not my wish that the weak should have harm done him by the strong, nor is it my wish that the strong should have harm done him by the weak.

The right, that is my desire. To the man who is a follower of the lie I am no friend. I am not hot-tempered. What things develop in my anger, I hold firmly under control by my thinking power. I am firmly ruling over my own impulses.

The man who is cooperative, according to his cooperation thus I reward him. Who does harm, him according to the harm I punish. It is not my wish that a man should do harm; nor indeed is it my wish that if he does harm he should not be punished.

What a man says against a man, that does not convince me, until I hear the sworn statements of both.

What a man does or performs, according to his ability, by that I become satisfied with him, and it is much to my desire, and I am well pleased, and I give much to loyal men.

Of such a sort are my understanding and my judgment: if what has been done by me you see or hear of, both in in the palace and in the expeditionary camp, this is my capability over will and understanding.

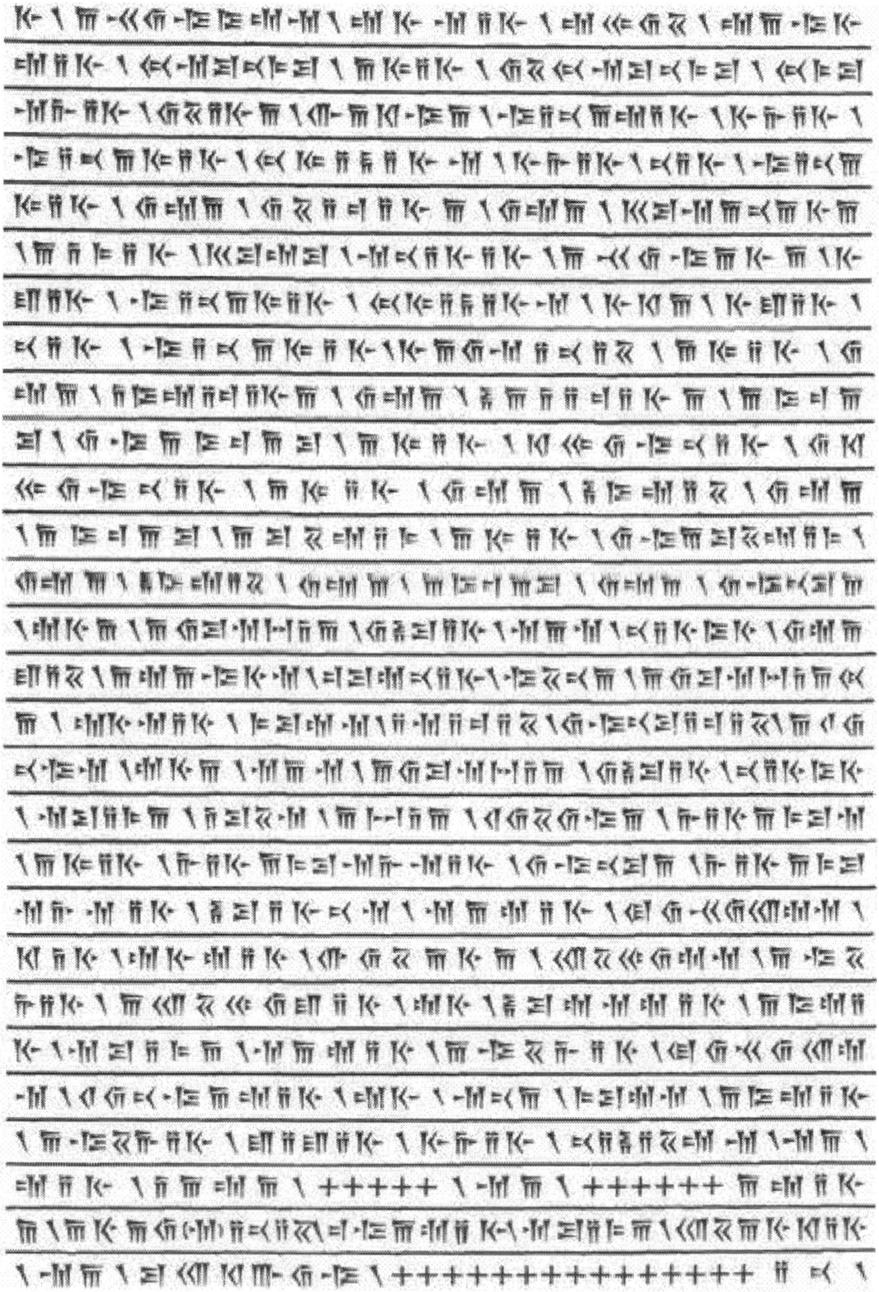

33. y \ aruvastam \ tyamaiy \ tanûš \ tâvaya

34. tiy \ hamaranakara \ amiy \ ušhamaranakara \ hakara

35. mciy \ ušîyâ \ gâthavâ \ vainâtaiy \ yaciy \

36. vainâmiy \ hamiçiyam \ yaciy \ naiy \ vainâ

37. miy \ utâ \ ušîbiyâ \ utâ \ framânâyâ

38. \ adakaiy \ fratara \ maniyaiy \ aruvâyâ \ ya

39. diy \ vainâmiy \ hamiçiyam \ yathâ \ yadiy \

40. naiy \ vainâmiy \ yâumainiš \ amiy \ u

41. tâ \ dastaibiyâ \ utâ \ pâdaibiyâ \ asabâ

42. ra \ uvâsabâra \ amiy \ thanuvaniya \ utha

43. nuvaniya \ amiy \ utâ \ pastiš \ utâ

44. \ asabâra \ ârštika \ amiy \ uvârštika \

45. utâ \ pastiš \ utâ \ asabâra \ utâ \ ûvnarâ

46. \ tyâ \Auramazdâ \ upariy \ mâm \ nîyasaya \ utâ

47. diš \ atâvayam \ bartanaiy \ vašnâ \ Auramazdâh

48. â \ tyamaiy \ kartam \ imaibiš \ ûvnaraibiš \ aku

49. navam \ tyâ \ mâm \ Auramazdâ \ upariy \ nîyasaya

50. \ marîkâ \ daršam \ azdâ \ kušuvâ \ ciyâkaram

51. \ amiy \ ciyâkaramcamaiy \ ûvnarâ \ ciyâkara

52. mcamaiy \ pariyanam \ mâtaiy \ duruxtam \

53. thadaya \ tyataiy \ gaušâyâ \ xšnnutam \ avaš

54. ciy \ âxšnudiy \ tya \ partamtaiy \ asti

55. y \ marîkâ \ mâtaiy \ avašciy \ duruxta

56. m \ kunavâtaiy \ tya \ manâ \ kartam \ astîy

57. \ avašciy \ dîdiy \ yaciy \ nipištam \ mâ \

58. taiy \ dâtâ \ +++++ \ mâ \ ++++++âtiy

59. â \ ayâu(ma)iniš \ bavâtiy \ marîkâ \ xšâyathiya

60. \ mâ \ raxthatuv \ ++++++++++++++ina \

This indeed my capability: that my body is strong. As a fighter of battles I am a good fighter of battles. When ever with my judgment in a place I determine whether I behold or do not behold an enemy, both with understanding and with judgment, then I think prior to panic, when I see an enemy as when I do not see one.

I am skilled both in hands and in feet. As a horseman, I am a good horseman. As a bowman, I am a good bowman, both on foot and on horseback. As a spearman, I am a good spearman, both on foot and on horseback.

These skills that Ahuramazda set down upon me, and which I am strong enough to bear, by the will of Ahuramazda, what was done by me, with these skills I did, which Ahuramazda set down upon me.

O man, vigorously make you known of what sort I am, and of what sort my skillfulnesses, and of what sort my superiority. Let not that seem false to you, which has been heard by your ears. Listen to what is said to you.

O man, let that not be made to seem false to you, which has been done by me. That do you behold, which has been inscribed. Let not the laws be disobeyed by you. Let not anyone be untrained in obedience. *[The last line is unintelligible]*

Source: *Livius*. Articles on Ancient History

INDEX

Abbasid, 39, 42, 43, 51,
Abu Bakr, 26
Abu Muslim, 35, 39, 40
Achaemenid dynasty, 14
Adam Smith, 73, 74, 87
Adam Tokar, 90, 143
al-Ash'ari, 49
Aleppo, 55
Alexandria, 31
al-Mamun, 45
Al-Muthanna ibn Harithah, 26
al-Zahir, 56
Anoushiravan, 23
Anthony M. Kennedy, 88
Arianna Huffington's, 98
Armenian, 20
Asharite, 49, 50, 52, 53
Assyria, 18, 19

Baghdad, 42, 44, 47, 48, 52
Basra, 29, 35, 36, 37, 39, 49
Beit al Hakam, 46
Bill of Rights, 92, 94, 95, 96,
161, 165, 168
Biruni, 50

Buyid, 42, 48, 49
Carthage, 32
caste system, 23, 28, 33, 34, 37,
41, 48
Christopher Pierson, 74, 76,
147
Church of the Holy Sepulchre,
32
Columbus, 67, 68, 75
Constantinople, 32, 43, 71, 72
Croesus, 28
Ctesiphon, 25 31, 52
Cyrus the Great, 24, 27, 38, 54,
79, 162, 163

Damascius, 39
Darius, 24, 35, 37, 38, 39, 53,
55, 79, 163, 164, 179, 181
darvishes, 48
David Kotz16, 103
dehghan, 42
Diffusion of Innovations, 40

Egypt, 32

Estakhr, 37
Eurocentrism, 24

Farabi, 56, 115
Ferdinand II, 75
Ferdosi, 31
fiqh, 41, 50, 61, 66, 67

garrison towns, 37, 38, 40, 41,
42, 43, 44, 45, 46, 48, 50, 52
Ghadesieh, 44
Ghazali, 60, 61, 62, 64
Granada, 68, 75
Gujarat, 49
Hasan of Basra, 43

Heilbroner, 78, 148, 156
Heraclius, 32
Hira, 32
hub cities, 50, 52

Ibn Rushd, 64
Ibn Sina, 58, 63
Imperialism, 21, 69
Isabella I, 75

Jerusalem, 32
Jess Krannich, 96
Joseph Schumpeter33, 110

Kavadh, 33
Khalid ibn al-Walid, 34
Khavarej, 48
Khorasan, 47, 53
Khosrow Parviz, 32
Khwaja Nizam al-Mulk, 60
Khwarizmi, 53, 55, 56
Koran, 45, 52
Kufa, 37

Locke, 79, 83, 88, 149, 157
Louis XIV, 77

madhhabs, 59, 60
Maury Klein, 108, 152
Max Weber, 51, 76, 147
Maximum, 90
Mazdakite, 31
Mecca, 33
Medina, 33
Mercantilism, 51, 78
modernity, 12, 52
Mongol, 64, 65, 66
Montesquieu, 79, 80, 81, 83,
84, 85, 88, 148, 157
Morrison R. Waite, 95
Mu'tazilah, 44, 45, 46, 52, 54,
57, 61
Muhammad, 33

Naemon, 32
Nahavand, 44
Neo-Babylonians, 27

Nizam al Mulk's, 62
Nizamiyyah, 60, 63

occasionalism, 57, 61

Pantia, 28
Paul Stevens, 96
Persepolis, 30
Plato's Academy, 21, 38, 39, 43, 44, 46, 52
pursuit of pleasures, 54

Razi, 56
Reza Shah, 24, 25, 71
Ridda, 33
Rogers Curve, 40
Rousseau, 79, 83, 88, 149, 158

Sasanian, 30
Sergius, 33
Shafi'i, 61
Shah Abbas, 66
Shahanshah, 51, 56
Shahrbaraz, 32
Shapur, 31
sharia, 9, 61, 62, 63, 64, 66, 67, 71, 73
Sharia, 23, 63
Shia, 47, 49, 51, 56, 59, 66, 67
Shiraz, 37

Shybani tribes, 32
Sufis, 49
Suhrawardi, 63, 64
Sunni, 42, 59, 61, 66
Sunnite, 42
Supreme Court, 86, 90, 91, 95, 97, 149

Tabuk, 34
Taif, 34
taqlid, 58
Thomas Friedman15, 102
Tilley, 136, 152, 158
Timur, 65

Umar, 37
Umayyads, 47, 51
Ummah, 33

Valerian, 31
Western civilization, 22
Westphalia, 77

Xerxes, 30

Zoroastrian, 49, 53, 55

Kamal
707 789 9092
707 338 4455 cp
Kamalazari @ Gmail .cw

Made in the USA
Charleston, SC
29 May 2014